Raspberry Pi Ideas Book

Discover a New World of Possibilities to Build and Develop Original Projects & Programs (Step-By-Step Updated Guide)

By

Ethan J. Upton

Table of Contents

Introduction 1

    Raspberry Pi Anatomy 1

Chapter 1 - Testing the Raspberry Pi as a Virtual Machine 2

    Stay Current: Keep Raspberry Fresh Via Update 2
    Network Coupling: VMware and Raspberry Pi 3
    Restore Network Connection 4
    Using Keyboard Settings 4
    Surf More Comfortably And Retrofit Your Browser 4
    Necessary Accessories For Raspberry Operation 6
    Micro USB Cable And Power Supply 6
    Screen And Raspberry: HDMI, CVBS or Nothing 7
    Raspberry Pi: DIY In Two Minutes 8
    The Case: Build Yourself Or Buy 8
    Plexiglas Housing For Easy Mating 9
    Creative And Colorful: Lego Housing From The Toy Box 10

Chapter 2 - Setting Up And Configuring Raspberry Pi 11

    No Screen Connected? - Fix Boot Problems 11
    SD Cards: The Difference Between Fast And Slow 12
    Select Image and Install on SD Card 13
    Commissioning: Root Or Pi? 14
    Windows: The USB Image Tool In Use 15
    Backup With The USB Image Tool 15
    Transfer Image To The SD Card 15
    No Witchcraft: Fdisk In Use 16
    Deleting And Creating Partitions 17
    Checking And Partitioning The SD Card 17
    Save And Activate Partitions 17
    Adjust The File System Again 18
    Tuning Measures For The Raspberry Pi 18

Overview Of System Utilization With htop..........................19
Optimization By Memory Splitting...19
Command Line Fetishists: Stop GUI Startup......................21
Configure Swap File In Fstab 22
Optimize Files And Directories Via Fstab 22
Reduce Consoles 23

Chapter 3 - Step By Step To The Perfect System...24

Customize Console Settings..24
Adjust Console Settings 25
Console Basics: Important Commands At A Glance...........26
Chmod: Effective Permissions..28

Chapter 4 - Raspberry In The Network...29

Practical And Secure: Access Via SSH 30
Debian Squeeze: Turn On SSH...30
No Installation Required: Windows Access Via PuTTY 31
Practical And Clear: Switch On PuTTY Full-Screen Mode..31
Switch Off Raspberry Pi With A Mouse Click 32
Mac OS X: SSH Access Through The Built-In Console.......32
Retrofit WLAN Adapter: Attention, Chipset!......................33
Download And Install Driver..34
With Certainty: Defining Network Settings 34
Commissioning WLAN 35
DHCP: IP Address Searched...36
Accessing The Raspberry Pi File System Via The Home
Network..37
Pair Mac OS X with Raspberry Pi via Samba 39
Change NetBIOS Name 41
When The Mac Denies Access..41
Be Careful When Accessing The Macintosh HD 42
Share Windows Folder For Raspberry Pi In The Home
Network..42

Chapter 5 - Living Room PC 3.0: Smart TV Self-Made..........................45

OpenELEC: Load Or Compile? 45
Download And Customize The OpenELEC Image..............46
Commissioning A Finished OpenELEC Image 46
Getting, Compiling And Installing OpenELEC 47
Preparing To Compile 47
Prepare SD Card For OpenELEC..49
Transfer OpenELEC To The SD Card 51
Larger Memory Card?...53
Setting Up The XBMC Media Center....................................54
Administration Via The Command Line: Enable SSH Access
....57
Setting Up Samba: Convenient Access To The Mediacenter
....57
Access To NFS / Samba Shares In The Home Network 58
Weather Forecast With The Weather Plug-In 61
OpenELEC: Reduce High CPU Utilization..........................62

Chapter 6 - Raspberry Pi Practice: Projects And Solutions..........................66

Automatic AirPrint Installation With Python Script 83
Password Protection When Printing....................................84
Jack As Standard Output Device For Audio 89
Setting Up Shairport 91
Uses: Webcam and Raspberry Pi...92
Obtain And Compile FFMpeg...93
Install Zone Minder Via Apt-Get..98
Apache Fine Tuning and Bug Fix 100
Pair IP Camera with Raspberry Pi......................................106
Commissioning the IP Camera 107
Pair IP Camera with Zone Minder 111
Zone Fine Tuning: More Bandwidth, More Quality 113
Electronic Watchdog On The Raspberry Pi 114

Conclusion........................118

What Is It Possible To Do With A Raspberry Pi?...............118

Description........................120

What Is Raspberry Pi? 121
Who Is The Raspberry Pi Book For? 121

Introduction

Congratulations on purchasing *Raspberry Pi 4: Project Ideas Book,* and thank you for doing so.

There are plenty of books on this subject on the market, thanks again for choosing this one! Every effort was made to ensure it is full of as much useful information as possible; please enjoy!

Raspberry Pi is a very small (credit card-sized) microcomputer. A few years ago, some members of Cambridge University and some English computer scientists decided to team up to form a foundation called the Raspberry Pi Foundation with one goal: to increase the number of computers available to children. They knew, however, that it would be necessary to create low-cost, programmable equipment priced at $ 25, the equivalent of a textbook. The main objective of the development team was to stimulate the teaching of basic computer science in schools.

In 2012, the credit-card-sized microcomputer was launched at $ 25, which naturally piqued the interest of the hardware, programming, Linux and beyond community...

Raspberry Pi Anatomy

Currently, Raspberry Pi comes in two versions - model A and model B. Both are the same size. The difference is in model B, which has one more USB port, has an ethernet port, and 512MB of RAM, unlike model A which has only 256MB of RAM. The processor is a 700MHz ARM, equivalent to the processor used in many of the smartphones in the market. It does not include any internal memory. However, it has an SD card slot.

Chapter 1 - Testing the Raspberry Pi as a Virtual Machine

After downloading, unzip the file into its own directory and either start the corresponding RaspberryPi.vmx file (VMware) or the RaspberryPi. ova file (Oracle Virtualbox). In this case, the virtualization software is automatically started, which takes the selected image into operation.

Here, of course, the virtual Raspberry does not have a "real" hard disk, but a "virtual" hard disk on the computer - nothing more than a container file set up by Virtualbox or VMware, then as a "hard drive" for the virtual machine, in this one Case Raspberry, to serve.

After starting the virtualization environment, log in to the virtual Raspberry Pi for the first time. Usually, the corresponding user name is pi - the corresponding default password is raspberry (all lowercase).

Switching off the Raspberry Pi via the console is done simply via the command sudo init 0 or via the graphical user interface. In this book, unless explicitly stated, the VMware image will be used to implement the Raspberry Pi in the virtual machine.

Stay Current: Keep Raspberry Fresh Via Update

Basically, it would not matter which version the operating system of the Raspberry Pi has in the used image. Because, assuming a fast broadband Internet connection, the operating system is brought up to date in a few minutes via command line.

Update the operating system and the installed applications - in theory: Who - like the author - has decided to use the VMware image, will encounter the first hurdle after the first start of the virtual machine: The network for the Raspberry Pi is not available.

The reason: The required eth0 network interface was not available on the Raspberry Pi. To correct this error, the Raspberry Pi virtual must be touched up manually. Once that's done, get the mentioned commands to bring the Raspberry Pi up to date.

Network Coupling: VMware and Raspberry Pi

Basically, you have several options for bringing the virtual host and the physical computer together in terms of network or to include the virtual host in the domestic network. The most widely used variant is Bridged Mode, in which the virtual machine gets its own IP address from the DSL / WLAN router in your home network.

The NAT (Network Address Translation) mode, in which the virtual machine and the physical computer share the IP address, so to speak, is technically possible, but the problem is the other way round - that is, if you have a connection from the outside or another computer in the home network with the guest record, is first time troubleshooting announced to find out why the connection does not work right away.

Therefore: Use the bridge port of the virtualization software - whether you use the Oracle or VMware product.

Restore Network Connection

Delete the so-called Mac address cache. The network interface is now available, which can be checked via the ifconfig command in the console. Subsequently, the update of the system via sudo apt-get update nothing in the way.

Using Keyboard Settings

Anyone who has used one or the other Unix command in the console of the virtual Raspberry Pi, may have noticed in the specification of parameters or options, that what it says on the keys, and what arrives in the console, a Small is little different - that is, a wrong configured Tasta-Tureinstellung is active. Who would like to use the German keyboard setting including use of the umlauts in the console, which gives in the console first the command:
sudo dpkg-reconfigure console-setup to start the configuration of the console.

Surf More Comfortably And Retrofit Your Browser

Here you will find tens of configuration pages, all of which are converted to German / German. For reasons of space, we did not print all of these here.

If you are unsure about an option, just keep the default settings. The settings made become active immediately after completing the wizard.

Depending on the Raspberry Pi image used in the virtual machine, an Internet browser is also available. But even old acquaintances such as Mozilla Firefox and Google Chrome (Chromium) can be retrofitted in a few simple steps:

You start the Google Chrome port with this command:
sudo apt-get install chromium browser
To install Mozilla Firefox use the command
sudo apt-get install firefox
No matter which browser you want to use: Less is more, you can best set up just one browser for space reasons.

After starting the link, the installed web browser appears on the smart Raspberry Pi interface in the virtual machine.
Working and trying out the Raspberry Pi in the virtual machine is, of course, only half as exciting compared to the »real« Raspberry Pi - the use of the credit card-sized board is only really interesting in practice. If you have already informed yourself in advance about the Raspberry Pi on the Internet, you have probably already read that there are different revisions here.

Development continues not only in IT in general but also in the Raspberry Pi project. Every few months there is a development on both the software and on the hardware side to report: While the first Raspberry Pi, Model A, with only one USB port and no network connection was delivered, was the successor, model B, already with equipped with two USB ports and one RJ45-10 / 100-Mbit network interface.

In autumn 2012, the model B was replaced by a second B model (revision v2), which is equipped with more memory compared to its predecessor. While the first models are equipped with 256 MB of capacity, the B2 model now offers 512 MB - twice as much RAM.

Necessary Accessories For Raspberry Operation

In the time you wait for the delivery of your Raspberry Pi, you can get an overview of the existing and necessary accessories for commissioning the device. Depending on the intended application, this accessory is very different, since the Raspberry Pi is very flexible.

For example, the Raspberry can be configured with screen output via the existing HDMI output or via the CVBS socket, but also operate without a connected monitor is possible. This is especially useful if the Raspberry is to quietly and unobserved to perform his service, for example, as a controller for a security camera or a doorbell.

In any case, the power supply that is made via a micro USB socket on the Raspberry Pi board is imperative.

Micro USB Cable And Power Supply

Mini vs. Micro: With the almost unmanageable plug and corresponding variety of sockets on the USB port, the Raspberry is in need of the slightly flatter micro USB cable than the mini-mini, which is mainly used in mobile devices such as smartphones and navigation systems. In terms of power supply is for the stable operation of the Raspberry Pi, a 5-W power supply (5 V, 1000 mAh), the right one. Here we have misused the surrounding power supply (5.4 V, 1000 mAh) of a Garmin Nüvi 3790 T since, in our case, this is only used in the car anyway.

Because of the micro-USB port and the low power consumption are especially power supplies from the mobile phone accessories market.

When buying a similar power supply can be so quoted around 5 euros - preferably in a communication dealer as niebauer.com who also useful additions such as fast SD memory cards, Bluetooth mobile keyboards also be used for the Raspberry Pi let mini-screens etc. has in his assortment. So, if something should not work, you have the advantage of being able to make representations there immediately - including exchanges -; in the case of an anonymous provider via the Internet, the e-mails will only be sent back and forth.

Screen And Raspberry: HDMI, CVBS or Nothing

For connection to a screen, the Raspberry Pi offers an HDMI connection and, alternatively, a so-called CVBS connection. Depending on the intended application purpose, the operation without a connected screen is possible, such as for the control of a bell system or video surveillance, etc., if the Raspberry Pi should finally do tax or control tasks.

Apart from multimedia use via OpenELEC, where the Raspberry Pi is directly connected to the TV via HDMI connection, the Raspberry Pi is perfectly suited for background services such as AirPrint, AirPlay, etc. and comes here without screen and keyboard.

Whereas powerful computers used to be housed in a sturdy metal cage with low-noise fans, today's generation of minicomputers, such as the Raspberry Pi, comes without any active fans and is even sold without a housing. But just for visual reasons, the purchase of a suitable housing makes sense. Other offerings such as passive heat sinks for the Raspberry Pi, on the other hand, recall the days of the cheapest backyard workshop, when the computers were still assembled cheaply by self-appointed specialists.

Long story short: save the money and invest it better in a matching power supply. For a new Raspberry Pi costs just under 34 euros, the heatsink with 8 euros plus shipping amount to more than a quarter of the price. Even if the seller here promises an increase in performance in the description text, the question arises, where the well should come from - as well as the question of the quality of the adhesive film, especially if one remembers the dangling processor fans in earlier PC times.

Raspberry Pi: DIY In Two Minutes

Depending on the purpose and personal preference, the small, check-card-sized Raspberry Pi board is operated by the hard-core without any protection in the form of a housing, etc. Depending on the location of the board and possible weather conditions, this is not only not advisable, but a housing may even be mandatory. Be responsible enough and use a suitably sized and safe solution for your application. The Raspberry Pi Forum, in particular and the Internet, in general, abound, providing ideas and examples of DIY or assembling a case. It only takes a little time and creativity to create a personal gem for the Raspberry Pi.

The Case: Build Yourself Or Buy

If you do not have a creative self-builder, you can use the junk-zone of the internet in the auction houses and look for a fitting case from the numerous providers. Here, pay particular attention to the type designation for the Raspberry Pi case - although the Raspberry Pi models are almost identical, but the number of connections varies depending on the model A / B1 / B2, and this also affects the case and the jacks out. It can be assumed that the successor models are similarly compact and clearly designed.

Basically, the Raspberry Pi can be operated without housing due to the small and robust design. However, depending on the purpose and location, you should still think about the use of a housing - especially when the Raspberry Pi is placed in the living room on the TV, and small children's fingers in the household go on a journey of discovery.

Plexiglas Housing For Easy Mating

You get dirt cheap housing in the market - there is no doubt about that. Like everything else in the world, a decent case has its price. This starts with the look: the cheaper a case is, the more boring it usually looks. The choice of the right housing depends mainly on the purpose and of course on the price. Basically, the prettier and the better the processing, the higher the price. For a good compromise in terms of price and appearance, in this case, provide transparent Plexiglas plates.

Good housings for the Raspberry Pi have a lot to offer in terms of ease of assembly. The PCB is then clamped in a housing holder, which you simply put together for easier assembly and which also makes a robust impression otherwise.

With the Plexiglas solutions for the Raspberry Pi, you have to deal a little more gently with the clamp closures, because a leg is broken off quickly. This is not bad at first, because there are three more that hold the case together. But you should not disassemble and assemble the housing too often. This is usually not necessary because the better housing the Raspberry Pi ports cut out accordingly, and thus they can be used comfortably.

Creative And Colorful: Lego Housing From The Toy Box

If there is still a box of Lego bricks left in the basement of the son, and if dusting away, the purchase of the Raspberry Pi is an opportunity to knock down the dust from the box and build a suitable housing with the existing Lego bricks.

Here you can let your creativity run free: When assembling the Lego bricks simply the places for the respective connections - power supply, depending on the application USB and / or LAN or HDMI / CVBS output for connecting the screen - off.

Chapter 2 - Setting Up And Configuring Raspberry Pi

After assembling the Raspberry Pi and refueling the SD card with the desired image for the new »computer,« it is put into operation. Before you go ahead and place the SD card in the Raspberry Pi, you should at least know the configuration parameters for the Raspberry Pi in order to tailor the small minicomputer to the intended purpose. The configuration parameters are defined in the text file config.txt, which is located in the boot directory of the Linux distribution used. After switching on the Raspberry Pi via the power cable, it is read at system startup and interpreted accordingly. If, for example, no screen is used on the Raspberry Pi, this should also be set accordingly in the config.txt file.

No Screen Connected? - Fix Boot Problems

No sound after switching on the power cord? The case occurred when the first start of the Raspberry Pi when it came to take this without a connected screen in operation. During the initial setup you should connect a USB keyboard, and a screen to at least enable the SSH server function. This allows the Raspberry Pi to be conveniently remotely administered with the computer via SSH.

Open this file directly on the memory card and use a Unix-compatible text editor that works correctly in terms of line breaks and character encoding. While you can handle onboard resources from Unix-based operating systems such as Mac OS X, you better use editors like Notepad ++, Primalscript, or

UltraEdit, which are all highly recommended. Here you look in the file for a possible culprit - in practice, once for the HDMI screen, output changes are necessary if no screen is to be connected. In this case the option hdmi_force_hotplug = 1 has to be set - in this case comment out.

SD Cards: The Difference Between Fast And Slow

If the Raspberry Pi still does not start, you should take the used SD card out of the Raspberry Pi and inspect it more closely. The reason: not every SD card can be used with the Raspberry Pi with any operating system - here; there are different experiences.

If you read on the Internet in numerous forums on the subject of Raspberry Pi, you have the impression that the selection of the right SD card is a game of luck nowadays: Here is the widespread opinion that you can minimize the risk of a bad buy only then if you avoid the faster cards, which usually have capacities larger than 16 GB.

In addition to the classic SD cards with capacities from 8 MB to 2 GB, there are cards that either use the SDHC technology (SD 2.0) with capacities from 4 GB to 32 GB or the SDXC technology (SD 2.0) with capacities between 48 GByte and a maximum of 2TB are equipped.

For the Raspberry Pi, especially the SDHC cards come into question - not least for cost reasons. Basically, SDHC cards are divided into different speed classes, which are also printed on the cards. That is, a class 6 labeled SD card has a write speed of at least 6 MB per second. In contrast, the reading speed can not be determined directly from the speed class. In most cases, it is well above the specified minimum write speed, and higher-end models usually achieve higher read speeds than lower-rated SD cards.

The use or selection of the correct SD card depends primarily on the intended use of the Raspberry Pi: In our case, we set a Class 10 for the Raspberry Pi in connection with the OpenELEC project Sandisk Extreme with 16 GB, which has been in continuous operation for three months.

On another Raspberry Pi, which provides network services on the home network, however, is a slower 8 GB Class 4 card in use. For the use of the Raspberry Pi with a space-heavy Zoneminder installation, however, an 8 GB card is again the minimum - but here you have many directories and data outside the SD card, for example, the USB port, to a USB port. Stick or reconfigured on network shares; this can be more than sufficient again.

Select Image and Install on SD Card

The speed check is particularly useful if you have several flash memory, speak SD cards, available, all in terms of capacity for the Raspberry Pi are sufficient, but you do not know which of them is the fastest. Since the published operating system images for the Raspberry Pi require a 2 GByte card and therefore hold correspondingly large partitions, this size should represent the lowest minimum. The prerequisite for this benchmark are administrator rights under Windows.

For the selection and installation of the appropriate operating system for the Raspberry Pi, the steadily growing network community provides suitable images that you can try free of charge and without obligation. The download addresses of the various operating system images for the Raspberry Pi are listed in the table below.

At first glance, the beginner does not understand what lies behind the respective distribution and multimedia center compilation. Even hardcore, advanced Linux pros find it hard to gauge the differences in XMBC builds. In addition, every user has their own preferences, but with the use of the Raspbian / Debian image on your Raspberry Pi, you will not be wrong at first.

Every few weeks, new versions of the image files are published on the relevant Raspberry Pi pages, such as www.raspberrypi.org - in this example; we used the Wheezy-Raspian package dated 16.08.2012. This can be later updated during operation in a few moments - the downloading and installing the image on the SD memory card is, therefore, a one-time thing.

Commissioning: Root Or Pi?

If the operating system is freshly installed and no keyboard and language customizations have yet been made, the initial login will be done with the default user and default password, which varies depending on the operating system used.

If, for example, the SSH server on the Raspberry Pi is initially deactivated, a direct login to the Raspberry Pi is also possible, provided that a keyboard and a screen are connected.

Because of the default US keyboard, the letter "y" of the raspberry password on the connected German keyboard is still on the letter "z." In this case, use the password raspberry. No matter which image or operating system you use - after logging in to the Raspberry Pi for the first time, you change the password of the user with the password command, which ensures greater security during operation.

Windows: The USB Image Tool In Use

A similarly convenient command-line tool as dd from the Unix world is unfortunately not available for Windows. To transfer the image file to the SD card under Windows, the USB Image Tool is available here. The tool itself requires the DotNet (.Net) environment under Windows, which should also be installed on a state-of-the-art Windows system. If not, you must first download and install .Net from Microsoft to get the USB Image Tool up and running can.

Backup With The USB Image Tool

After starting the program, select the USB drive in the left-hand pane and click on the backup button in the lower right corner. Note that the memory size of the memory card backup naturally also corresponds to the capacity of the inserted card. This may be a problem with memory cards larger than 4 GB if the backup is to be stored on an old file system.

Transfer Image To The SD Card

For example, to write the downloaded Raspian image to the inserted SD card data carrier, the Admin mode is also required under Windows. If you have not already done so, start the USB Image Tool in Admin mode by highlighting the file and using the context menu of the right mouse button to select Run as administrator. Then select the extracted operating system image of the Raspian system by clicking on the Restore button.

After writing the image file, do not remove the memory card yet, first quit the USB Image Tool, and then safely remove the hardware. There, select the SD card data carrier or the corresponding drive and end the operation of the SD card by clicking on the OK button.

SD cards are now available in countless different capacity and speed classes, and meanwhile, more or less 4 or 8 GB SD cards are standard equipment. For compatibility and especially for space reasons, the Raspberry makers provide the appropriate Debian / Raspian image in the (unpacked) size of 2 GB, which, as described above, also on a larger memory card with 4, 8 or 16 GB can be transferred.

No Witchcraft: Fdisk In Use

In the first step, you select the used memory card - in this case it is device mmcblk0. Use the following command to enter the fdisk command mode:

sudo fdisk / dev / mmcblk0

Now you are in your own fdisk console. Entering the letter m gives you an overview of the available commands at any time.

Now let's start by outputting the current parameters of the installed memory card with the command p:

Now the two available partitions are displayed on the SD memory card. Here is the order of the sectors, which are counted in ascending order. The Raspberry Pi image has a fixed FAT32 portion (from sector 8192 to 122879) mounted as the / boot partition, as well as the actual Linux partition that begins immediately after sector 122880.

The goal is, therefore, to enlarge the Linux partition. This is where the FAT32 partition remains, the Linux partition is first deleted and recreated with the old sector start limit. The value of the end sector, of course, depends on the new size - but more on that later. First, delete the Linux partition of the memory card.

Deleting And Creating Partitions

They do not really erase the data, just change the partition limits for the memory card. In this example, there are two partitions. The second partition is the Linux partition. For deletion, in this example, first, enter the letter command d (delete) followed by the partition statement 2.
In the next step, you enter the new partition limit for the Linux partition.
When creating a new partition, first tell fdisk with the n command that you want to create a new partition. Since this is a so-called primary partition, then enter the associated command p for it. The partition number is calculated automatically, but can also be adjusted. In this example, the same number 2 is used for the partition number as for the already used Linux partition.

Checking And Partitioning The SD Card

On the one hand, you take over the partition limits from the "old" Linux partition - because you left the first partition unchanged, the boot sector of the second partition remains the same as 122880. To specify the end sector of the second partition, use the default entry, which depends on the available memory card size. In this example, this is the value 7744511 - which here corresponds to the full capacity of the 4 GB SD card.

Save And Activate Partitions

Now, the changes to the partition limits have been entered in the fdisk console but not yet activated and saved. This is done with the w (write) command - but if you do not want to save the changes made, use the q (quit) command to exit the fdisk console.

After exiting the fdisk console, you start with the command and sudo reboot the Raspberry Pi new. If necessary, the file system must be rearranged and repaired after the restart so that this, too, can handle the changed capacity.

Adjust The File System Again

After rebooting the Raspberry Pi and logging into the console, use the Resize2fs command to customize the file system:
sudo resize2fs -p / dev / mmcblk0p2
The 2-parameter -p used in the example is used to display the progress bar when customizing the file system.
At the end of the procedure, check on the console whether the memory space on the Raspberry Pi has really grown: Use the command df -h to list the memory space of the active partitions.
The capacity specification for rootfs or / dev / root is informative: In this case, you should have nearly double the capacity in the case of a 4 GB SD card.

Tuning Measures For The Raspberry Pi

After a while, any computer is too slow, including the Raspberry Pi. But with the Raspberry Pi you have the disadvantage that you can not simply add additional memory or a faster CPU - the compact design makes a hardware-side expansion impossible , What remains are the interventions in the Kernel and operating system beginnings, also the optimization of the Linux file system can bring here a few percent additional resources. In effect, how fast the Raspberry Pi will feel depends on the purpose and amount of services and programs installed on the Raspberry Pi. However, the tips below provide for performance enhancements here and there.

Overview Of System Utilization With htop

Before you blindly and luckily make any system or configuration changes, you should first learn in principle, where the bottleneck is in the system: With the appropriate tool, you will learn which processes how many resources need. Then you can decide whether you want to run one or the other program instead of another computer or even install additional services and programs, should there still be enough CPU time and memory available. If not already available, install the tool htop by command:
sudo apt-get install htop
After starting htop, the memory and CPU-intensive processes are listed in descending order. Depending on the service in progress, the information is constantly changing, but for a basic assessment this is more than sufficient: If a process over a longer period, for example, a continuous CPU time of over 90%, either the Raspberry is too weak, or the process is On the best way to operate the Raspberry Pi at the stop. Here, if necessary, the reconfiguration of the memory allocation of the Raspberry Pi will help.

Optimization By Memory Splitting

Basically, the file start.elf specifies the distribution of the total memory available on the Raspberry Pi between main and graphics memory for the operating system. After the basic installation, Debian / Raspian's / boot directory contains different files with the extension * .elf. No matter how many of them are in the directory - only the file start.elf is used and evaluated when starting the operating system. By default, this is configured for a Raspberry Pi with a total of 256 MByte on an allocation of 192 MB of memory for the RAM and 64 MB for the graphics memory (Debian).

Then there are 224 MB available for the main memory (RAM) for which Video memory (GPU) 32 MB. After rebooting, the Raspberry Pi is the changed division then active.

If you have a Raspberry model with 512 MB of total memory in use, you can also change the allocation:

RAM graphics VRAM use case 256 MB 256 MByte GUI usage, many applications with video features, Playing and decoding, streaming, XBMC, mandatory for Full HD 1920 playback.

384 MB 128 MByte GUI usage, many applications with video capabilities, Playing and decoding, streaming, XBMC, mandatory for Full HD 1920 playback.

448 MB 64 MByte In principle, no GUI usage recommended, no playback videos, no hardware video acceleration, exclusively providing network services.

496 MB 16 MB Absolutely no GUI usage is recommended as well as none playing videos, no hardware video acceleration, exclusively providing network services.

Since October 2012, the allocation of memory via the corresponding files is a thing of the past. These are then no longer available in the / boot directory - only the well-known files start.elf, and start_cd.elf as well as fixup * .elf are allowed with the new firmware. Here the distribution is controlled by a parameter in the configuration file config.txt. By specifying gpu_mem = 16 assigns the graphics memory size of 16 MB. The values permitted here are between 16 and 192 MB for a 256 MB RAM Raspberry, and for the 512 MB model the permissible range is 16 to 448 MB. The rest of the memory not allocated to the graphics card is automatically used as RAM memory.

Command Line Fetishists: Stop GUI Startup

Depending on the operating system used on the Raspberry Pi, you have a different approach. Basically, you use the raspi-config command to set the basic installation of the Raspberry Pi . Here you check that the switch boot_behaviourstart desktop on boot? set to No. If you would like to start the graphical X11 interface later from the text-based terminal, simply do so via the command startx in the console.

If so, modify it to use the execute privilege per sudo chmod 644 /etc/init.d/slim remove, or remove the slim package completely from the Raspberry Pi with the command sudo apt-get purge slim.

Support Memory: Create Swap File

Especially for systems with a small amount of memory, the setup of a so-called paging file or a paging memory brings a big plus in performance. Especially when many services and programs are active, they require more memory than physically available. For example, in order for the operating system to operate flexibly, Linux does not work directly with the physical RAM, but rather with the virtual main memory, which consists of the physical RAM and a defined memory area on the hard disk. Here, the virtual memory on the hard disk is provided by the swap partition or as a swap file.

To create a so-called swap file on the Raspberry Pi, open a file and use the dd command to write in as many bytes as the swap file should be large. The swap file must then be formatted with the mkswap command. Finally, activation takes place in the system via swapon command.

In the next step, you integrate the created swap file into the file system of the Raspberry Pi. This requires an intervention in the system file fstab.

Configure Swap File In Fstab

Basically, you will find in the / etc / fstab file all volumes or the corresponding partitions that should be automatically mounted when the Raspberry Pi starts up. To open and edit this file, root privileges are necessary. With the command
sudo bash
nano / etc / fstab
Open the configuration file and comment out the / var / swapfile entry if it already exists in the fstab file. In this case, remove the leading picket fence icon (#). If the entry does not yet exist, enter it - the spaces between the entries / values are set using the [Tab] key.

Since the fstab file is currently open on this occasion, you can also stop saving the access time of a file or to a directory on the Raspberry Pi, which can bring a small burst of speed.

Optimize Files And Directories Via Fstab

The data partition of the SD card is also entered in the fstab file so that it is available to the operating system after starting the Raspberry Pi. Here you also add the nodiratime parameter in the line after the defaults, noatime entry. Basically, it is by default that Linux stores the last access time of a file (atime). For Raspberry Pi use this information is usually not

needed - even the time of accessing a directory is uninteresting, which can bring here a small burst of speed.
After the change, you save the file, but the tuning action will be active after the restart of the Raspberry Pi.

Reduce Consoles

For miser: If you want to further optimize in terms of storage needs, turn off the file a few more consoles - usually no more than two are needed. Open the file for this
sudo nano / etc / inittab
and comment there with the picket fence symbol (#) the getties 2 to 6:

Chapter 3 - Step By Step To The Perfect System

If you want to put a perfectly tuned Raspberry Pi into operation in your home network, you can configure your system as it is necessary after installation. Since the Raspberry Pi does not have a BIOS or EFI compared to a computer, it works with configuration files and many parameters. Therefore, it is necessary to learn something and apply different Linux commands in the console. This is the only way to directly influence the existing programs and services, the customization of the language settings and the keyboard, but also later to set up the network and much more.

Customize Console Settings

If the Raspberry Pi does not display a configuration menu after the first start, you can do so by entering
sudo raspi-config
Start manually to make the initial setup. If you have loaded the American keyboard driver, you must use the [ß] key instead of the hyphen key since the wrong keyboard setting is currently active. After starting raspi-config, navigate with the arrow keys and the [Tab] key in the text-based user interface. First, adjust the console settings and set here via the menu item the default settings of the localization.

If the terminal is now converted to the German language and the UTF-8 encoding, check the set keyboard layout of the Raspberry Pi. In the main menu of raspi-config, select the item configure_keyboard. If you connect to the Raspberry Pi mainly via SSH, the selection of the keyboard tur Generic 105-key (Intl) PC recommended.

To change the keyboard layout to QWERTZ, select Other in the following dialog to go to the language selection. There you navigate with the arrow keys to the entry German and select the OK entry with the [Tab] key.

In the subsequent dialog, select German again, and after confirming with OK, a dialog will appear in which you can define the function of the [Alt_Gr] key on the keyboard. Here, as well as in the configuration of the so-called ComposeKey, you keep the default settings.

Last but not least, you can use the keyboard shortcuts [Ctrl] + [Alt] + [Back] as a key combination to quit the X server. Make sure the switch boot_behaviour start desktop on boot? set to No. If you would like to start the graphical X11 interface from the text-based terminal later, simply use the command startx in the console.

Adjust Console Settings

For the changes to take effect, quit the raspi-config menu by choosing Finish and start in the following dialog on Would you like to reboot now? by selecting Yes, the Raspberry Pi new. If you want to reboot later, you can do so with the command

sudo reboot

If the US keyboard on the Raspberry is active again after the reboot, check the settings of the configured keyboard with the command

sudo dpkg-reconfigure keyboard-configuration

To subsequently make changes to the localization and time zone on the console, you can use the commands

sudo dpkg-reconfigure tzdata

sudo dpkg-reconfigure console-setup
use to directly start the appropriate configuration.

Console Basics: Important Commands At A Glance

The console or, in the case of Linux and Mac OS, the terminal comes in text mode by default and can also be started from the window manager. So that Linux newbies also feel right at home on the command line, here are the most important commands at a glance:

Description command
Ends the specified running kill process
Execute command as superuser sudo [COMMAND]
Change user usermod [USER]
Add Users useradd [USER]
Delete user userdel [USER]
Copy file cp [filename.extension] [TARGET] /
Delete file mv [filename.extension]
Find file find -name "[filename.extension]"
Move file mv [filename.extension] [TARGET] /
Show file content less [filename.extension]
Services on the Raspberry Pi terminate service [service name] stop
Services on the Raspberry Pi start service [service name] start
Restart services on the Raspberry Pi service [service name] restart
Find out DNS information host
Editor nano nano [path] [filename]
Ctrl key and X to save and exit
Editor vi vi [path] [filename]
Esc key and: q to save

i-key for changing / inserting text
Creates links between files and folders ln
Show free space df -h
Unpack GZ archive gunzip [filename.gz]
Help on individual commands man [COMMAND]
Stop running processes and shut down the system shut down
Show list of active processes ps -ax
List of previously entered commands history
Show
Description command
Find MAC address arp -a
Display network configuration ifconfig
Delete folder rmdir [FOLDER NAME]
Change Folder cd / [FOLDER NAME]
Show folder contents ls or ls -al
Change password passwd
SSH connection to remote computer ssh [IP address] or:
take ssh [DNS address]
When changing user the desired user names before [IP address] or [DNS Address]: ssh_benutzername @ [IP address]
Unzip TGZ archive tar xzvf [filename.tgz]
Shows the current location in the lwd folder
Displays the hostname to hostname
Displays the path of a program

For more information about a command, it's best to use the man mechanism. With the man command (from manual, manual), the console throws out the appropriate syntax with parameters for almost every console command. For example, typing cp will list all the parameters for copying the file / folder.

Chmod: Effective Permissions

A specialty in Unix, in general, is the chmod command. The Unix rights system has three different areas:
- user
- Group (group)
- Other (other)

The following properties can be assigned for each area:
- r = readable, value: 4
- w = writable, value: 2
- x = executable (executable), value: 1

On the Linux of the Raspberry Pi, for example, if you run ls, properties are displayed in the following format:

rwxrwxrwx

The first three letters are for the user domain, another three are group, and the last three are for other. To get the representation in the form of an octal number, you have to add all values for each range. In this case: (4 + 2 + 1) (4) (4) = 744. So you can use

chmod 744 [FILENAME.DATE EXTENSION]

set the appropriate rights.

Chapter 4 - Raspberry In The Network

If you want to bring the Raspberry Pi in the home network and the Internet, it must be a cable to the distributor (router) shot. If this is not the case, you can also create a network connection by radio. All you need is a suitable WLAN adapter for the Raspberry Pi.

It does not matter which network interface you are using, by default, the Raspberry Pi has a DHCP client active that obtains its network parameters from the Dynamic Host Configuration Protocol (DHCP) server in your home network. Not only does DHCP provide the IP address, but it also lets you automatically set preferences for the DNS server, gateway, netmask, domain, and more with the help of options.

The IP address of the Raspberry Pi can be assigned statically but dynamically, depending on the MAC address of the computer. In short, the Raspberry Pi gets its IP address and associated network settings assigned automatically.

Control Raspberry Pi via SSH: PuTTY, Terminal & Co. In Use

Particularly secure access to Unix-based systems is not only possible via a so-called secure, encrypted connection, but also urgently recommended over the Internet for security reasons. Access via the WLAN interface is even more so. Thus, not only is the WLAN generally safer thanks to a secure router configuration with the use of WPA / WPA2, but also the access via SSH provides additional security so that unauthorized persons can not make nonsense on the target computer. Once SSH access is set up, you can access the system and user data on the target computer, copy data back and forth, and much more, depending on the user.

Practical And Secure: Access Via SSH

A Raspberry Pi does not require peripherals such as a mouse, keyboard, or screen to operate, and because of its flexibility, it is also of great interest for out-of-the-ordinary places. If you want to administrate comfortably from the desk or the sofa, you will appreciate the SSH functionality. This makes it possible to get the remote command line on the local computer as if you were sitting directly in the garage in front of a connected screen with a keyboard.

After the Raspberry Pi has been switched on for the first time, a configuration dialog appears, in which the start of the SSH server can be lashed so that it is available after each power-on. Then you can connect to any client over the network using the secure SSH protocol with the Raspberry Pi.

Debian Squeeze: Turn On SSH

The choice of operating system with the Raspberry Pi depends mainly on the future purpose and the associated functions: For example, who instead of Debian Wheezy (Debian 7) still uses the predecessor Debian Squeeze (Debian 6) can easily in the first partition of the SD Reboot the boot_enable_ssh.rc file in boot.rc to turn on SSH functionality (FAT32 / boot partition).

After plugging into the Raspberry Pi, the built-in SSH server is activated and can now be accessed as usual via the home network with a suitable SSH client. Some operating systems not only bring a built-in SSH client, but also a built-in SSH server, and then it is possible to access non-Unix- based operating systems like Windows. However, this also requires the installation of an SSH client.

No Installation Required: Windows Access Via PuTTY

If you have not already done so: Download an SSH client program to the Windows PC for secure access to the Mac. PuTTY is a real pleasure for purists of the command line, who would rather work in the window world, for which stands with WinSCP (www.winscp.com/), a suitable tool at the disposal.

Practical And Clear: Switch On PuTTY Full-Screen Mode

Especially in the beginning, when setting up the Raspberry Pi you work a lot on the console until the Raspberry Pi is set up as far as you wish. Especially when restarting PuTTY, it is annoying to constantly set the window to the desired size with the mouse - here, the full-screen display is much more useful. These can be used with the key combination [Alt] + [Enter] with activated PuTTY and thus also back to the window mode.

[Alt] + [Enter] is not activated, you can also start the PuTTY full-screen mode by right-clicking on the title bar of the terminal window.

To enable full-screen mode by default, select the Behavior entry in the left pane of PuTTY when it is started and then activate Full screen on Alt-Enter. If this is not only valid for the current, but also for all other terminal windows in the future, save the setting in the Session area. There, under Load, save or delete a stored session, select the entry Default Settings and then click the Save button.

For an existing saved session, however, the customization does not count. Here you must first load the corresponding profile, activate the key combination as described above, and then save the profile again.

Switch Off Raspberry Pi With A Mouse Click

On the above download page of PuTTY you will also find an additional program called plink.exe. You place this in the same directory in which the program putty.exe is already stored. In the example below, both the putty.exe file and the plink.exe file are located in the C: \ directory of the Windows hard disk.

echo off

c: \ plink.exe -ssh -pw openelec root@192.168.123.47 poweroff

exit

Then save the file with a descriptive name and the file extension .cmd. The file can also be stored in the same directory as the PuTTY tools - this requires a desktop link to the cmd batch file. Alternatively, create the cmd file directly on the Windows desktop. Now save yourself from logging in and shutting down the Raspberry Pi.

Mac OS X: SSH Access Through The Built-In Console

Unlike Windows, the SSH client is already included in Mac OS X. So only the opening of a terminal window via Programs / Utilities / Terminal is necessary, then can be by command

ssh root @ IP ADDRESS

to access the target computer. After entering the password, the file system of the remote station is available. For those who prefer a bit more convenience, get the freeware Cyberduck, which lets you drag and drop files and entire directories from the Mac to the target computer.

Before connecting, configure Cyberduck with the SFTP protocol and input the IP address of the Raspberry Pi on the server. Alternatively, if configured, use the DNS name of the remote site. The default SSH port setting is 22 and does not need to be changed. For username, you use the account that is available to you for the target computer - if password is the corresponding password.

Retrofit WLAN Adapter: Attention, Chipset!

Once the SSH access has been successfully established, you can switch and act as you wish: The main area of application via the SSH console is the remote maintenance of the target computer, which can now not only be accomplished quickly but also thanks to the encryption used goes.
Ubuntu: Retrofit SSH Access
Similar to Mac OS X, the SSH client is usually included on Linux systems. But sometimes it comes with extremely slim configured Linux derivatives that it must be installed after.

New operating systems adapted for the Raspberry Pi have included built-in kernel driver support for USB WLAN adapters since October 2012, based on the Realtek chipset (RTL8188CUS and others).

If you are planning to use a WLAN adapter on the Raspberry Pi, you should make sure that it is equipped with a Realtek chip - the RTL8188CUS - when purchasing the WLAN adapter.
Here you can then use the plug-in card without further ado and configure it directly with the appropriate WLAN tools or the configuration parameters via the network setting of the Raspberry Pi. Basically, with the Komman-dos lsusb and

dmesg you can find out which devices are currently active on the USB bus.

When using lsusb -v, the built-in chip is usually also displayed in the WLAN adapter. If not, you can continue to research using the device ID - which comes in the 1234: 1234 format.

Download And Install Driver

On the other hand, if you do not want to or do not want to switch to a new firmware or operating system, you can still install the WLAN USB port manually. After restarting the Raspberry Pi, restart the script:

After the actual driver installation, which is done automatically by the script, the network settings for the wireless network have to be defined.

With Certainty: Defining Network Settings

After integrating the WLAN interface in the Linux configuration - here it is available as an interface under wlan0 - this must be configured. Here, the script inter alia queries the SSID and the access password for the wireless router, if access to it (hopefully) secured by a secure WPA2 password.

After selecting the encryption method, enter the name of the SSID to be used. These entries can be adjusted later if necessary and are stored in the network / interfaces. The script then scans the WLAN environment and searches for the appropriate wireless network.

If the network parameters are entered correctly and the wireless network is initialized correctly, these parameters are saved.

Commissioning WLAN

Now the script has come to an end, as it were - you still have the choice, whether the Raspberry Pi should be brought up to date in terms of operating system and firmware or not. Select this option, but you may need to re-run the WLAN configuration after rebooting the Raspberry Pi to keep it enabled.
After using the easy system and operating system update option of the script after the WLAN driver installation and configuration, the setup WLAN may not be available after restarting the Raspberry Pi.
You simply check this in the console with the command ifconfig, which then outputs all active network interfaces. If the entry wlan0 is missing here, the following workaround helps for one-off users:
After the update, start the installation script for the WLAN adapter again and navigate through the individual points. All you need to do is to confirm or skip the parameters already set, such as SSID, encryption, etc. Also, the start of the system and operating system updates are not necessary. Run the script to the end - until the command prompt is available again in the console. Afterward, the WLAN configuration is saved and is available again after a restart of the Raspberry Pi.
Pull the LAN cable before the WLAN stick test. If the WLAN does not work, this usually has a trivial reason. So if you want to try out your WLAN stick, you should pull the LAN cable before starting the Raspberry Pi.
Just to run the Raspberry Pi on the net and use it to surf the web with multiple computers or from the couch, a home network would be a shame. You'll quickly see how convenient it is to share data between multiple computers, print jobs from one central printer, share digital photos with everyone on the

net, and more. This is all feasible with onboard resources. Also, safety aspects are not too short. However, you need a few basic requirements for smooth operation. In order to exchange data in the home network with other computers, the following prerequisites are necessary:
• TCP / IP installed.
• Working group established.
• Computer name entered.
• One or more computers have at least one folder or drive shared.
• Shutter names without umlauts, special characters and spaces, and no more than twelve characters.

For this to work, in addition to the IP configuration of the DSL router, the network parameters must be properly installed on each computer. This means in plain text that on each computer, a network adapter (network card, AirPort / WLAN card, etc.) is present and installed.

DHCP: IP Address Searched

When the Raspberry Pi is freshly unpacked and installed, its network interface is configured by default for DHCP (Dynamic Host Configuration Protocol) access. DHCP has its advantages, especially in large networks. This means that all computers connected to the router, regardless of whether they are WLAN or not, are automatically assigned the TCP / IP configuration. Manufacturers usually recommend not to change these settings and to use the domestic DSL / WLAN router as a DHCP server. DHCP, the dynamic allocation of IP addresses in the network, is both a blessing and a curse.

First of all, it is practical for every network newcomer not to have to worry about assigning such IP addresses.

If you have only a few computers to supply you with your router, it is often more sensible and safer to disable the DHCP server in the wireless router and manually configure the connected clients. Not only do you have an accurate overview of which computer is on the network with which IP address, but also make it more difficult for a potential intruder to "grab" an IP address in your home network.

If there is no DHCP server or DSL router in the network that is responsible for the automatic assignment of the IP addresses, the IP addresses and the subnet masks must be entered manually for each computer. The choice of the IP address is up to you. For a better overview, you should always ascending an address with 192.168.123.1, 192.168.123.2, etc. awarded.

In a home network, the Raspberry Pi is usually integrated with the Ethernet interface. Friends of wireless pleasure use Wi-Fi via a small Wi-Fi adapter, which they still have to get extra. No matter which of the two ways you go, the IP configuration is almost identical for both interfaces. Despite DHCP, you can also reserve an IP address for a computer in the LAN by selecting DHCP with manual address.

This will always give this computer the same IP address when accessing the DHCP server. This is particularly the case with highly available computers and servers, which often require permanent IP settings, for example, because port forwarding is active in the DSL / WLAN router - this has also proven to be extremely favorable for the Raspberry Pi in practice.

Accessing The Raspberry Pi File System Via The Home Network

Anyone who has a Mac or a Windows computer in their home network, in addition to the Raspberry Pi will eventually want to transport data from A to B and back. To access the Raspberry Pi file system or individual directories conveniently from home computers the installation and configuration of the Samba package is necessary. Samba is included in almost every Linux distribution; it only needs to be selected during installation.

With Samba, the Raspberry Pi behaves like a Windows server for the computers on the network. If Samba is optimally configured, you can later create your own log-in profiles for all users and user groups. These are then stored in a directory on the Raspberry Pi and exported as a / netlogon directory. The Windows clients then automatically use the appropriate log-in scripts. Basically, you can copy the contents of the file printed here. Only the global entries for netbios name, server string, and workgroup should be adjusted.

First, create the smb.conf file that controls the Samba configuration for the Samba configuration. This belongs to the Raspberry Pi with Debian in the directory / etc / samba and has several blocks, each containing variables for configuration can be set. Each block represents a release in principle, with two areas of particular importance. The most important of these is the [global] section that sets the general Samba settings.

In the [homes] section, a user who accesses the Raspberry / Debian server from another computer is provided with the home directory on request. This requires an entry in the smbpasswd file. Via smbpasswd -a NAME, create a Samba user in the / etc / smbpasswd file:
sudo smbpasswd -a pi

Now enter the password of the user pi and confirm it. Subsequently, this user can be used under Samba. This admittedly unfriendly double administration effort for the user passwords, you can turn off with a small intrusion into the smb.conf:

unix password sync = yes

However, the most important entries are already present in the printed smb.conf.

With the command ps fax | grep smbd check if the samba server is really running. If not, you may find a typo or syntax error in the smb.conf file. With the Samba test program testparm you can easily and safely check the Samba configuration for possible errors.

Fortunately, if the testparm program issues error messages, it also indicates the line number of the line in which the error most likely occurred. In this case, please correct the corresponding lines in the smb.conf file. If the configuration goes through, you have made the first part, congratulations! To be on the safe side, restart the Samba daemon:

sudo service samba restart

If you already have a computer in the home network in operation, you can see the Raspberry Pi in the network environment after restarting the Samba service. Now check the Samba user configuration on the computer.

Afterward, the corresponding shares are visible in the Explorer. If you wish, you can assign a separate drive letter to the network drive under Win-dows using the command Map network drive.

Now you can access the Raspberry Pi from all computers in the home network - of course, that is also possible.

Pair Mac OS X with Raspberry Pi via Samba

If you do not want to go the cumbersome way via an FTP / HTTP server in the home network, you better use the direct route via a Windows share as described above. But the reverse approach, namely accessing the Raspberry Pi to a configured Mac share, is also possible after some setup work on the Mac.

1. In the first step, make sure that the workgroup name of all machines in the network is the same. On the Mac, you open the System Settings Network and here the WINS tab. In the current example, the workgroup is called workgroup first.

2. Another basic requirement is that the corresponding checkmark in File Sharing is set via System Settings / Sharing. The Device Name input box displays the NetBIOS name of the Mac computer that you set in the System Preferences Network on the WINS tab.

3. To configure Windows-to-Mac communication, first make sure the user names are the same on Windows and Mac OS. Here also on request, click on Create a new user account on the plus icon with just a few clicks, which can be used to access the folder to be shared.

4. The New person window appears. Input the user name and the corresponding password. Click on Create account to create the Mac user.

Ideally, you will use the same password as on Windows - in this case, you will save yourself the hassle of password access on Windows.

In order for the logon or the access from a Windows PC to work, a corresponding directory for access must be defined in the user settings of the user active under Mac OS X, here the directory Public.

5. By default, Mac OS X initially supports only Apple's proprietary Apple Filing Protocol (AFP) for data access to the Mac. In order to grant the Windows world access to the Mac hard disk, you must explicitly allow and set up Windows access here.

In contrast to its predecessors, Mac OS X version 10.5 and higher no longer has the Windows File Sharing switch; the Windows share via Samba is hidden under options in File Sharing. Then select the user account or accounts that are allowed to use Samba access.

6. Last but not least, under Sharing, set the access rights:

7. Now switch to your Windows computer and check the network environment to see if the Mac is visible. If not, restart Windows or press the function key [F5] to refresh the view. Double-click the Mac icon to access the shared Mac directory.

Change NetBIOS Name

The NetBIOS name for the Mac machine is grayed out in the dialog box and can not be changed there. If you want to use a different name, you can change it under System Preferences / Sharing. When the NetBIOS and Workgroup names are configured, the Samba configuration is complete.

When The Mac Denies Access

But for many users, nothing happens. Although the Mac can be seen in the Windows network environment, Windows reports a network error while trying to access it. The solution can be found in the Mac OS X firewall settings. For security reasons, many users have their firewall settings set to allow only necessary services.

1. For Windows to be able to access the Mac, you must enable the option Allow all incoming connections for the first access. The File Sharing service (AFP, SMB) is automatically displayed. After that, you can change the firewall settings again.
2. When you click your Mac icon again in the Windows Network Neighborhood, the Connect to <COMPUTER> dialog box appears. Enter your username and password here. Confirm with OK.
3. The shared Mac directory is displayed in the Windows Explorer, and the flow of data between Mac and Windows - and thus also to the Raspberry Pi - nothing stands in the way of Mac OS side.

Be Careful When Accessing The Macintosh HD

Depending on whether read access and write permissions have been assigned under the system for access, it is important to pay attention here: Since Samba also displays the system folders and files (hidden in Mac OS X) in addition to user data, You should be careful when editing or deleting files. Too big a risk of destroying the user profile on Mac OS X.

Share Windows Folder For Raspberry Pi In The Home Network

The release of a folder under Windows is done in a few clicks: You open the Explorer and select the folder to be shared with other users on the network. Right-click on this folder and in the context menu, right-click Release for. Below is a dialog in which you can set up access to the folder.

Then the configured folder share is active. The user who has been set up for access can now access the set release from another PC in the network - provided that the name and password are set up in the user administration of Windows.

The removal of an established release and a subsequent change are analogous. Here you select the corresponding folder in the Explorer and select Properties or better in the context menu. On the tab Sharing, you get an overview of who can access the folder and which rights or permissions are set up for the different users.

If you would like to remove a created share, deactivate the checkmark in the field Share this folder in the dialog box Extended Release.

Subsequently, access via the network is no longer possible. If the Samba share of the Raspberry Pi becomes a problem when accessing via the Windows Explorer or the directory contents are not displayed, the following tip will help.

Windows Zips When Accessing Samba: Release Problems

If your home network has a Raspberry Pi with Samba, a NAS server (such as QNAP, Buffalo devices), a full-featured Linux / Samba server, and a Samba share for the Mac, accessing the network shares is usually easy if they can be seen in the network environment, and the corresponding access rights are available. That counts only for the first registration.

This annoying issue can be resolved with a small configuration change: Press the Start button, and then you need to type secpol.msc in the Run box. Then go to Local Policies and Security Options, where you can customize the following two entries.

Since neither the group policy editor (gpedit.msc) nor the editor for local security settings (secpol.msc) are included in the functionality of the simple "home user versions" such as Home Basic and Home Premium, you must use the Registry Editor are gone to the release problems when

Access to the NAS server or the Linux / Samba server in the home network to solve.

Open Network Shares Automatically In The Finder

If you have permanent access to your Raspberry Pi shares in the home network via a Linux / Windows / Samba server, then manually adding the share using the shortcut [Command] + [K] will be annoying over time.

It is more convenient if you automatically connect a shared share and display it in the Finder. Via apple / system settings / user / startup objects, add the desired share (s) as a so-called startup object. First, select the appropriate user, then select Startup Items in the tab and click the Plus icon.

If a password or other user ID, including password is required to access the network share, it is recommended to save the access information in the personal keyring. In this case, the access is established immediately, and the annoying password query is omitted. After the next login, these shares are automatically opened and displayed in a Finder window.

Chapter 5 - Living Room PC 3.0: Smart TV Self-Made

A flexible, powerful, and above all quiet computer in the living room requires special components. The days when chunky computers in mini and midi-tower format were used for smooth, smooth video file playback and Internet / home network access are over. Instead, use the small, fanless Raspberry Pi with the purpose-built OpenELEC system to play all the video and music files from all available video sources in your home network, as well as convenient access to the public Internet TV archives Broadcasters and foreign broadcasters who also publish their broadcasts on the Internet.

Last but not least, you will learn how add-ons can be used to comfortably browse video archives such as Spiegel Online, Süddeutsche.de, and others online and use them free of advertising - all from the comfort of your own couch. The TV broadcasters, in particular, offer a one-of-a-kind program around the clock: Reports, sports, documentaries, reports on current affairs - a completely new viewing experience at the click of a mouse and on-demand. Whenever you want to see the program, it is immediately available.

With the Raspberry Pi in conjunction with Open Embedded Linux Entertainment Center - OpenELEC for short - you have an all-rounder in the living room that retains an overview of all media files in the home and ensures significantly increased comfort and a better selection in everyday TV life.

OpenELEC: Load Or Compile?

If you decide to use OpenELEC, you should also be aware that the installation and configuration of the multimedia functions in the Raspberry Pi are not rocketed science, but require a little time and patience, and above all, the will to occur To understand and solve problems yourself. Of course, advanced users have more options for influencing the configuration and composition of OpenELEC if the package itself - ie the system that comes on the SD card - is compiled and compiled. For those who have little or nothing to do with Linux, Terminal, Shell, and Perl scripts, it is recommended that you download and use a precompiled OpenELEC package.

Download And Customize The OpenELEC Image

No matter what size the image file comes in, it has a compressed file format in the form of a * .tar.gz or * .tar.bz2 file. While unzipping such files on Mac OS or Linux with built-in operating system tools is possible, you need help on Windows. Download the best of the free and completely sufficient for home use Packer 7-zip.

Which operating system image you choose is initially a matter of taste - in principle, of course, best an image file with a relatively fresh build date and - if different sizes for the target SD card are available - the right one to the existing SD card. In this case, you will save yourself from later adapting the OpenELEC installation to the actual capacity of the memory card.

Commissioning A Finished OpenELEC Image

At least during commissioning and initial setup SSH access to the Raspberry Pi system is recommended, but it is disabled by default in OpenELEC. However, SSH can be conveniently switched on when the XBMC is started or by creating an empty file named ssh_enable in the /storage/.config directory become.

Getting, Compiling And Installing OpenELEC

If necessary, insert the memory card into the computer again, mount the memory card in a Unix system and use the following commands in the terminal window to create the file:
cd /storage/.config
touch ssh_enable
If the card is subsequently plugged into a Raspberry Pi, the SSH server should be started when the OpenELEC is started up. If you have connected to the OpenELEC from a computer via SSH for the first time, change the password of the administrative root user (default: openelec) with a passwd command.
Basically, a real native Linux is recommended for compiling - just for speed and time reasons. If you do not want to have full-fledged native Linux on your computer, you can also prepare and run the installation on Mac OS or Windows using a virtual machine. Basically, you need a reasonably current Linux distribution, so you get the OpenELEC package compiled clean. There are a few special features in the game. As the target platform of the Raspberry Pi is known to be an arm processor architecture, the compiler on the Linux machine must dominate the so-called Cross-Compiling. In this example, we use an Ubuntu installation in a VMware virtual machine.

Preparing To Compile

In the example described below, we used an Ubuntu installation (12.04) under VMware Workstation 8 with the standard configuration. You need hard disk space for the translation - and that's not too tight: you should at least be able to provide around 9 GB of free capacity to prevent the compiler from stopping after about ten hours with an error message.

Also, the Linux in the virtual machine must be brought up to date - in order to be able to download OpenELEC in this case; you need, for example, the git package - specifically, the following packages and their dependencies were initially installed:

apt-get install git gawk build-essential gperf cvs texinfo libncurses-dev

xsltproc libxml-perl

apt-get install openssh-server

If you do not already have it, it makes sense to install an SSH server if you want to monitor the Unix machine remotely via the console. To be able to analyze and compile the downloaded sources, first, switch to the OpenELEC.tv directory.

cd OpenELEC.tv/

Then start in the subdirectory OpenELEC.tv with the command

PROJECT = RPi ARCH = arm make -j 8

Building the personal OpenELEC XBMC distribution.

In our example, after a relatively short time, an error message appeared - git criticized further missing packages on the Linux machine:

apt-get install gawk zip unzip xutils default-jre

Alternatively, in the absence of Java, the OpenJDK can be used instead of the default jre if you are developing on the Linux system.

apt-get install openjdk-6-jre

Anyway - start the compilation process by

PROJECT = RPi ARCH = arm make -j 8

again. After starting the compilation process, you can turn off the computer's screen - it will now spend several hours compiling the numerous packages, reloading other packages, and putting it together as a complete package.

Of course, it takes a bit longer to compile in a virtual machine than it did on a native machine: a VMware machine running Ubuntu 12.04, configured 1GB of memory, 20GB of hard disk capacity, and one CPU allocation Building the OpenELEC package in full configuration over twelve hours.

Also, the space required for the creation of the package is immense: Before starting, the hard drive was filled with about 3.3 GB - after compiling it was 8.4 GB more. For this reason, you should build the Linux machine and also pay attention to a sufficient hard disk equipment. Otherwise the compilation process in the dumbest case terminates shortly before the end due to lack of storage space.

After compilation, the result is stored in the directory OpenELEC.tv - here is a complete Linux distribution for the Raspberry Pi.

Prepare SD Card For OpenELEC

Like the customized Debian and Raspian for the Raspberry Pi, the memory card image for OpenELEC with two partitions must also be created on the SD memory card. However, here, OpenELEC separates like the FRITZ! Box - namely the operating system from the data area of the user -, while with the other derivatives only the / boot directory is pushed into the FAT32 partition.

Basically, the OpenELEC system with two partitions is split up as follows:

1. The first partition contains the FAT32 formatted / flash area of 128MB, usually labeled SYS or SYSTEM. In it are beside the files necessary for the boot process like
Bootlader and the like also the over 80 MByte SYSTEM file as well as the kernel.img file.
2. In the second partition formatted as ETX4, the user data is underlain. It contains the / storage area, in which not only the user data, but also XBMC Mediacenter settings, SSH settings, and much more will be saved. This partition is flexible, meaning that it does not matter whether you use a 4 GB, 8 GB, or 16 GB SD card - the storage space is also available in the / storage area.
If the SD card is plugged into the Linux computer or assigned to the virtual Linux machine, check with the command, for example
sudo blkid
or
udo dmesg
which device file the card is mounted on. In this example, it is / dev / sdb. So correct the address for subsequent commands, and possibly adapt it to your configuration. First check whether there are already partitions on the SD card.
Then unmount the SD card from the system - this is done by umount command:
sudo umount / dev / sdb
In the first step, the mentioned 128 MB FAT32 system partition is created for OpenELEC and in the second step it is marked as bootable.
Then, the second (data) partition is created, taking up all the space that is there on the SD card.
After a moment the changes are written. Now again check the (new) partitioning on the memory card with the parted command.

sudo parted -s / dev / sdb print all

If the partitions are created correctly, the next step is to format the partitions. The first, smaller partition is known to be formatted FAT32 (VFAT) while the data partition is populated using the Linux EXT4 format.

The system label is technically irrelevant - some call it sys or system, or storage or data in the partition of the data area.

To see the successful formatting of the two freshly created partitions now on the Linux system, re-initialize the partition table.

sudo partprobe

Now both partitions should be mounted in the Linux system. In the next step you transfer the compiled data to the SD card.

Transfer OpenELEC To The SD Card

The first step is to change to the command line in the OpenELEC.tv directory, which is usually also in the directory in which you have compiled OpenELEC.

cd ~ / OpenELEC.tv

Now check whether both partitions are properly integrated in Linux

- depending on the used Linux you have to help, many of them are already done automatically.

If you already want to use a pre-compiled OpenELEC, use the bootloader files.

The use of the arm128_start.elf file for the use of the 256 MByte memory ensures that both receive 128 MByte. Since only the start.elf file is interpreted at startup, in this case save the original file with a descriptive name and rename the arm128_start.elf to start.elf.

In the next step, a file called cmdline.txt will be added to the system partition, which will house parameters for the OpenELEC kernel.

The specification of disk = / dev / mmcblk0p2 indicates the data block, the specification of the ssh parameter ensures that the built-in SSH server is also switched on immediately after start-up in order to ensure remote access. The quiet parameter hides the startup messages after turning on the Raspberry Pi. For the first attempts, you can also supplement the debugging parameter if inexplicable errors occur during startup or operation.

OpenELEC-RPi.arm-devel - *. Kernel-

The boot logo is hidden by the nosplash parameter. After writing the cmdline.txt you now transfer the actual OpenELEC files - the kernel and the system.

When copying the system files, you should pay attention to the upper and lower case: The OpenELEC-RPi.arm-devel - *. System file ends up in the system directory of the SD card with the name SYSTEM, while the file is lowercase than kernel.img is copied there.

Finally, check again if all files have arrived on the SD card. The ls -latr / media / system command should look like this:

$ ls-latr / media / system
a total of 94078
-rwx ------ 1 root   root 2347220   2012-11-23   22:40 start.elf
-rwx ------ 1 root   root 17764   2012-11-23 22:41 bootcode.bin
-rwx ------ 1 root   root 88608768   2012-11-23   22:48 SYSTEM
-rwx ------ 1 root   root 5337008   2012-11-23   22:48 kernel.img

```
-rwx       ------ 1 root      root 50       2012-11-23      22:49
cmdline.txt
drwx       ------    2    root     root 16384    2012-11-23 22:49
..
```

You can unmount the two mounted partitions from the Linux system so that you can remove the memory card.

Now the time has come to plug the SD card into the card slot of the Raspberry Pi and put it into operation via HDMI on the living room TV. Note that the first boot process will naturally take a little longer, as for example

For the first time, things like the automatic setup of the swap file, the validation of the file systems or the generation of SSH keys must be done. The creation of the data structure for XBMC is also done on the first start of OpenELEC on the Raspberry Pi.

Larger Memory Card?

The memory card capacity fdisk solution only works with the described Raspian / Debian solution. In OpenELEC and other systems, this approach fails because the partition being modified is in use and can not be edited on-the-fly. For this reason, a Unix / Linux system or a matching virtual machine with a Unix / Linux system is necessary here so that you can extend the operating system image on the SD card to the actual capacity of the SD card if there are differences after transferring the system files.

In order to be able to use the inserted SD card with the Linux partitioning tool, it must first be unmounted from the system after being inserted, ie be unmounted. Only then is she available for full access. If GParted does not exist yet, install it by apt-get. With the command

sudo apt-get install gparted

sudo gparted

start the tool with root privileges. The use of GParted is self-explanatory: If the memory card is still in the card slot, it is still readable and writable by Linux, even if it is no longer mounted via file system in the Konqueror browser.

Select the memory card from the GParted drop-down menu on the top right - a good differentiator to the existing hard disk is, of course, the capacity of the SD card. Once the card has been read, an overview of the partitioning of the inserted SD card appears.

Now you only need to mark the "last" partition in front of the free space - marked with "not assigned" - with the mouse and in the context menu of the right mouse button select the item Change size / Move.

Setting Up The XBMC Media Center

After adjusting the memory size, click the Resize / Move button. In this case, GParted creates a corresponding work order, which must first be triggered. This is like processing a batch file - then start the directory operation from the menu bar with Edit / Execute All Operations.

If you would like to make the changes at a later time or not at all, select the item Delete all operations instead. Enlarging the partition is done in a few minutes. If the Linux system does not independently integrate the SD card or the two partitions into the operating system, the command sudo partprobe is sufficient in the terminal to mount the new partitions again under Linux. Now the enlarged partition should have been allocated the complete storage space. After unplugging it again and removing it from the Linux system, the SD card can finally be used in the Raspberry Pi with the full capacity.

The XBMC interface is, so to speak, the visible heart of OpenELEC. After switching on, the system boots directly into this interface - login with user ID and password is not necessary here. If your keyboard and mouse are connected to the Raspberry Pi, you can navigate with it for now. Wireless keypads are much more comfortable - there is a wide choice here, from the small Rii radio Bluetooth keyboards to the full-fledged 105-key keyboards, which can also be operated on a notebook, for example.

ssh_enable

In our case, we had an old, cordless Logitech diNovo edge keyboard lying around in the computer corner and even found the right little Bluetooth adapter. Plugin, try it - lo and behold: The keyboard is supported immediately by OpenELEC, another additional installation is not necessary here.

After connecting the keyboard, check the SSH access to the Raspberry Pi - unlike the »normal« Raspberry Pi image, another user and password must be used with OpenELEC / XBMC. Here you use the administrative user root for the remote access, as an initial password openelec is preset.

If you have not activated SSH access using the kernel parameter, the SSH connection is switched off in OpenELEC. But it can be retrofitted through the XBMC or through creating an empty file named in the directory /storage/.config can be conveniently switched on.

Once you have successfully completed the first connection, you can either continue to work with SSH or WinSCP, or you can set up a comfortable solution via Samba that can be easily accessed from your Windows computer via Explorer or via Mac OS via the Finder to the corresponding shared directories access the Raspberry Pi or OpenELEC and edit them.

For example, to turn on Samba support for accessing the OpenELEC system, you must first enable the Samba daemon on the Raspberry Pi. This is done when the OpenELEC is started via the XBMC interface.

Customize OpenELEC settings And Set Up Shares

While formerly netmount.conf needed to include network shares, XBMC now has built-in support for NFS (Linux), Samba (Windows), and AFP (Apple) access, which makes it easy to use the makes different media and storage locations in the home network much more comfortable. Selected operating system settings and their XBMC-related services can be conveniently changed via the Programs menu of the included OpenELEC OS Settings add-on. Start the corresponding option on the XBMC with a mouse click or [Enter] key of the keyboard.

Once the add-on OpenELEC OS Settings has been started, four tabs are displayed, which you can go through step by step and whose options you can adapt to your personal requirements. In the System tab, you first set the layout for the connected keyboard. If you have a QWERTY keyboard with umlauts, choose de for the layout (German) - for the alternative keyboard layout, for example, or one of your choice. Automatic updates are disabled in this example, with the use of an LCD screen can still make driver adjustments.

The Network tab contains the current network settings. Here are the parameters of the built-in, wired eth0 network interface. If you are using a WLAN USB plug-in module, this must be configured via the Network 2 tab.

In the Hostname field, enter the name of the Raspberry Pi as it should be called in the IP network or locally. However, this has nothing to do with the Samba server name that you may know from the Windows network. You do not need to change anything in the Network Adapter field unless you have a good reason to do so. Basically, OpenELEC is configured so that it can automatically be supplied with an IP address via DHCP.

Sometimes it may be useful to assign a static IP address to the Raspberry Pi. In the next step, you switch on the access functions to the OpenELEC Mediacenter. Before accessing the Raspberry Pi system via Samba or SSH, it must first be turned on and then configured.

In the Services tab, simply switch on the Start Samba at boot option with a mouse click or keyboard. A later Samba network connection from your computer uses exactly that authentication method, so make a note of the parameters.

Administration Via The Command Line: Enable SSH Access

If the cmdline-txt-gadget does not yet create the SD card image, the SSH access can also be switched on later via the XBMC interface. And last but not least, switch on SSH access with the OpenELEC add-on mentioned above - almost mandatory for administrative purposes in the home network.

Setting Up Samba: Convenient Access To The Mediacenter

Basically, make the changes to the Samba configuration in the /storage/.config/ directory. If this file is free of errors, the corresponding original will be overwritten and used in the / etc / directory. So you have in the file

storage/.config/samba.conf

If a personal, working configuration is stored for the previously activated Samba server, the default configuration of /etc/samba/samba.conf will be discarded when the Samba service is started, and the new file will be used.

The first access to the file is a bit tricky at first: After connecting via SSH, simply copy the sample file as a conf file in the console and open the created file with the well-known vi editor.

If you can handle the vi-editor, the workgroup, the NetBIOS name (netbios name), under which the shares in the Windows network are to be visible, as well as other parameters, such as additional shares, will be suitable. But also note here: Less is more - the main thing, it works first time a free-gift, but for right.

If you do not want to make any changes, or do not save them, use them to cancel the processing.

Access To NFS / Samba Shares In The Home Network

In order to be able to integrate remote shares from other computers on the Raspberry Pi or on the XBMC as if they were directly on the Raspberry Pi, you need a so-called mountpoint on the Raspberry. In principle, this is nothing more than a directory that provides the content of the network share virtually locally - namely, as long as they share in the home network can also be reached.

To do this, create in the writeable / storage area the directory or directories that should also be used in the XBMC. If SSH is enabled, connect to XBMC-Raspberry Pi and use the above commands, as in this example, two include Samba shares for video playback and an NFS share for additional music in the Raspberry Pi.

To access other Linux computers and NAS storage on a home network from the Raspberry Pi, this access must first be turned on and configured. While better NAS systems with RAID5 have a built-in graphical configuration menu in which the most popular types of sharing such as Samba, AFP (Apple File Protocol), FTP and NFS can be set up with just a click of a mouse, this is a self-built NAS or a Linux system a little less expensive. Here you enter the directory that you want to share in the network via NFS into a so-called export file.

This can be found in the / etc. directory - open it with an editor and enter the directory that should be released for the Raspberry Pi (or for other computers in the home network). As usual with Unix systems, a certain spelling of the share is necessary in this configuration file - here you are best guided by the self-explanatory sample entries.

The / var / nfs / music directory is only released for the IP address 192.168.123.47, behind which in this example, the Raspberry Pi is hidden. After saving the file, first activate the changes with the command

exportfs -a

Then leave with the command

exportfs

Show the active NFS shares of the computer.

The console command is sufficient on the Raspberry Pi with OpenELEC. Subsequently, the content of this directory is visible in the XBMC share / storage / music2 for the Mediacenter.

Better NAS systems for the SOHO area also bring the Windows release technology in the form of Samba - the access from a Unix system using CIFS (Common Internet File System) is possible.

In the following, it is assumed that a Samba and / or Windows share already exists in the home network. This is not a big science, even under Windows. Here you select the corresponding folder, right-click Properties in the context menu, click on the tab Sharing, and then on the button Advanced Sharing. Then enter a descriptive release name and click on the OK button.

The CIFS network protocol is based on NetBIOS over TCP / IP and SMB and is part of the Samba package. The integration of the Samba shares is done indirectly on the command line with the option -t cifs. Unhide the shares as usual on the command line using umount.

All commands can be entered after switching on the Raspberry Pi on the command line via SSH. But that gets pretty annoying when it has to be done manually every time you reboot. Therefore, for the Raspberry Pi insert and XBMC, a script is recommended, which is executed automatically after every start. This autostart.sh script is stored in the /storage/.config/ directory, it is structured like a simple shell script.

In this case, the network drive will only be mounted if it is not already mounted. The output of the mount command uses grep to search for the local approval name. If this is not found there, it is first checked by ping, if the remote computer is even reachable. If so, the mount directory is created via mkdir -p (if not available), and finally the mount command is triggered. In the example
mount -t cifs //192.168.123.123/USBDisk1/storage/videos3 -o username = xbmc, password = raspi
the user xbmc with the password raspi is needed. On the other hand, if you have not set any user-level security on the Windows PC (access each one), the following command is sufficient:
mount -t cifs //192.168.123.125/!_musicvideos_YT/storage/videos3
If the script can not be executed after autostart.sh has been created, it should first be executed once via the chmod + x autostart.sh command.
vi autostart.sh

chmod + x autostart.sh
./autostart.sh

If the newly included directories are also exported to the home network via Samba by the Raspberry Pi, the last line ensures that the "new," personal samba.conf is reinitialized.

To access the XBMC web server, OpenELEC also offers web access, which allows remote control of the system. Thus, any device that has a simple web browser can also act as a remote control on the sofa if you do not have a keyboard nearby.

vi ~ / .xbmc / userdata / guisettings.xml
/ Web

In order to activate the XBMC web server via SSH on the command line, it is necessary to intervene in the guisettings.xml file. Open it with an editor and search for the string Webserver - in the vi-editor / webserver in command-mode.

If that's too complicated for you, you can, of course also make this adaptation on the television via XBMC. Navigate via SYSTEM / Settings / Services / Settings to the web server menu:

The basic Samba configuration is also stored under XBMC. Here you should at least customize the workgroup label so that the default releases of XBMC can then be deployed on your home network.

After changing the settings, they should also become active. Here, XBMC usually requests a system reboot. By selecting Yes, this will be done immediately.

After restarting the Raspberry Pi, you can check on a computer whether the web server is running and whether logging in to the XBMC user interface is also possible.

An alternative browser like Firefox does not show this behavior and presents the web frontend of XBMC after entering username and password.

Note that you should only let the web server run if you really use it. Due to the limited resources of the Raspberry Pi, it makes sense to operate only the most necessary services for better performance.

Weather Forecast With The Weather Plug-In

If you want to be informed about the weather and the forecast for the next few days with every system, you can also activate the weather plug-in on the Raspberry Pi.

Seriously: The Raspberry Pi is more than busy with the XBMC, here we have also disabled the RSS treadmill in addition to the weather plug-in, so as not to permanently run the built-in CPU at 100% CPU utilization.

OpenELEC: Reduce High CPU Utilization

If you follow the discussions on the Internet in the OpenELEC forums on the most frequently encountered problems and demands, the topic of CPU utilization and memory utilization is on the top of the list. Here are the standard answers are always the same: disable unnecessary services, disable features such as weather frontend and RSS notifications - but the CPU load seems to remain high unabated.

Help is, however, a tip from an XBMC developer to draw attention in the right direction - as on a web page (http://thepcspy.com/read/how-fix-idle-100-cpu-issue-xbmc/) described on this topic. The reactivation of the so-called Dirty Regions should help to noticeably reduce the CPU load. If activated, only the changed menu areas will be recalculated, instead of rebuilding the entire menu on the screen.

If you are using the Samba configuration described in this book, you can easily access the network share /storage/.config via Windows Explorer, Mac OS X Finder, or other file managers. There you create a file named advancedsettings.xml. You can also do this via SSH in the console:

nano /storage/.config/advancedsettings.xml

Of course, you do not have to type the file completely. Download the file as a template from the OpenELEC project page and customize the entries.

Now restart XBMC and check if the created xml file is processed and used. In our case, we found only a slight decline in CPU utilization to 88% - not quite the resounding success. Incidentally, this was due to the fact that the resolution remained unchanged at 1,920 x 1,080. This should also remain so, since in the home network over the Raspberry Pi frequently HD streams must be transmitted and brought to the screen.

Spiegel Online, N24, Bild.de, YouTube, Süddeutsche.de and many more that present themselves on the internet and publish video material there, can also be integrated via XBMC as a video add-on. This will not only provide you with a clear overview of the videos of the corresponding offers, but also an advertisement-free and therefore comfortable presentation and navigation. The video add-ons can be easily installed via the XBMC homepage via video / video add-ons.

After download and installation, the plug-in provides the selected website as a video source.

If, for example, you have activated Spiegel Online's extensive video archive as a video source, you can first look at the sections defined there and then dig deeper into the archive from there.

In this example, the category Sport was selected by Spiegel Online, most of which was created in cooperation with the football magazine Kicker. There you will be informed daily about the events of the German Bundesliga and their clubs.

If different drives from other computers are mounted on the Raspberry Pi and also included as a share, the OpenELEC standard installation also provides the multimedia data such as pictures, videos and music in the home network for UPnP-compatible devices.

Playback of the media files over the network usually works smoothly - but when playing MPEG encoded material on the TV when playing back via the Raspberry, the screen remains black: Unfortunately, there is no indication - but in the Raspberry- Environment is well known that the Raspberry Pi simply lack the necessary licenses for MPEG playback. The subsequent purchase of the licenses makes the reproduction possible.

Submit MPEG-2 And MPEG-1 Codec

Only for the use of XBMC and omxplayer is the somewhat annoying option for playing video files that come in MPEG-2 or MPEG-1 format, here in each case the appropriate license for the decoder commercially available. These are obviously license costs that have to be paid to the MPEG organization.

To buy the right licenses, open the website www.raspberrypi.com. com / license keys /. Ordering requires the serial number of your Raspberry Pi - the code you received after the order expired. However, it is bound to the Raspberry Pi and must be specified for use in the configuration file of Raspberry Pi. To find out the serial number of Raspberry Pi, you need to open the command line via SSH and give the command

cat / proc / cpuinfo

on.

After a few hours or even several days, you will receive an e-mail containing your personal code for decoding the video files while playing. To make this code known to the Raspberry Pi or the XBMC, it is necessary that you edit the configuration file config.txt and enter the corresponding code in it.

You can either get the SD card out of the Raspberry and open the configuration file via the computer's SD card slot, or you can edit the file via SSH directly during operation. With a normal Raspberry Pi you open via SSH.

In the OpenELEC system, the file is stored in the read-only / flash area. Here you first open the / flash memory for write actions and then change the config.txt file. After saving the changes, reset the write protection for the flash memory.

Just add a new line for each codec and enter it like the example code below:

decode_MPG2 = 0x56781234,0x00001234

decode_WVC1 = 0x12345678,0x00005678

Sometimes Handy: Take Screenshots

For documentation purposes and the like, taking a screenshot of the XBMC is a welcome tool that you can easily make with your keyboard attached using [Ctrl] + [S]. If no keyboard is connected to the Raspberry Pi, but only a Spartan remote control in use, you need a command line connection via SSH.

Basically, the following command is required to take a screenshot on the OpenELEC system:

xbmc-send --host = 127.0.0.1 -a "TakeScreenshot"

Alternatively, the putty / plist tool can also be used to start a convenient batch file from the Windows desktop with a mouse click. The prepared screenshots will land in the / storage / screenshots directory on the Raspberry Pi.

Chapter 6 - Raspberry Pi Practice: Projects And Solutions

Anyone who owns more than one computer these days - be it because a new one has been acquired, be it because a second one is used at home or used by the children - will not be able to tackle the issue of networking at the latest by purchasing the Raspberry Pi , The Raspberry Pi shows its strengths, especially in network operation: Regardless of where you are and whether the data you want to access it on different computers and hard disks - the Raspberry Pi provides access.

With VPN: Secure Access To The Home Network

Anyone who wants to access the Raspberry Pi and thus his or her data in the home network without spies and credentials while away from home can also use the VPN functions of the home DSL / WLAN router. Especially a product like the FRITZ! Box from AVM basically offers this possibility, but still has to be set up and configured.

After that, nothing is in the way of secure access to the Raspberry Pi. You can upload or download data, configure and use things on the Raspberry Pi, and much more. In addition, not only the data access, but also the data transfer on a release basis is possible and extremely practical - for example, when the storage capacity of the digital camera on vacation is running low, and the data can be stored easily and, above all, safe on the local hard drive.

For this purpose, apart from the correspondingly configured DSL / WLAN router with VPN functionality, only one VPN client for Windows or Mac OS X is required, which is partially available free of charge. Based on the widespread FRITZ! Box, this practical application is described here - depending on the

DSL / WLAN router model with VPN functions, it can also be transferred to other models.

Setting Up The VPN Connection To The FRITZ! Box Home Network

In order to access the home network via VPN while on the move, a VPN-capable DSL / WLAN router and a special software VPN client on the notebook, Mac, or PC are required. No matter which VPN method or protocol - PPTP, L2TP, IPsec, SSL etc. - is used, both communication partners must use the same so that a connection is made. In most SOHO solutions the IPSec protocol is implemented, the corresponding key protocol ISAKMP / IKE provides the actual encryption of the connection.

In this post, the configuration of a VPN connection from a remote PC and Mac to a VPN-capable FRITZ! Box is explained by AVM. These DSL / WLAN boxes are distributed not only by AVM itself, but also by Internetproviders like GMX, 1 & 1 etc. Although the instructions refer to the original FRITZ! Box, they can also be applied to the OEM models. Basically, the following steps are necessary:

• Creating the configuration file
• Create the user-based access configuration file
• Import of the configuration file into the FRITZ! Box
• If necessary, install a VPN client and configure the VPN client using the FRITZ! Box configuration file

With the coupling of two nets the last step is omitted; here simply, the configuration file is loaded on both sides.

Create VPN Config File For FRITZ! Box

The FRITZ! Box receives its VPN configuration via a so-called config file in which the most important parameters for the connection are stored. In order to exclude typing and syntax errors here, AVM provides a wizard called FRITZ! Box Remote

Access Setup for creating the config files, which can be found on the AVM web server.

However, setting up the FRITZ! Box, remote access program, is only designed for Windows operation - if no Windows PC is available in your home network, an installed Windows XP or 7/8 on the Mac is via Boot Camp or Parallels or VMware Merger mandatory ,. Alternatively, the office PC can be used - only the setup wizard of AVM must be equipped with the appropriate parameters, the installation of the configuration files is done after work at home easily via the Mac.

After download and installation, start the program FRITZ! Box remote access. Before you get started, however, you should provide the following information for the VPN configuration - missing a trifle, the VPN connection will fail.

If you are on the Internet with a dial-up connection or a changing public IP address, you need a dynamic DNS address from a FreeDNS provider. Profiusers with a fixed IP address can use the IP address instead. Now an assistant opens - there select the option Configure remote access for a user and click on the Next button.

In the following dialog, enter the e-mail address of the user in the input field E-mail address of the user. This is the username, which does not necessarily have to be an e-mail address - you can also use any username. The wizard generates the password for this user name automatically.

In the next dialog, enter the dynamic DNS domain name configured in the FRITZ! Box in the Name field. Alternatively, an IP address can be entered - Power users with a fixed public IP address at home do not need to go through the dynamic DNS name.

If the FRITZ! Box in the home network uses the default configuration for the IP address range, use the option Factory setting of the FRITZ! Box for the IP network. In this case, the

FRITZ! Box provides the address range 192.168.178.0 for the devices in the home network.

On the other hand, if you have configured the IP address range according to your personal wishes, select the Use other IP network option and enter the IP network and subnet mask here.

In addition, enter here the IP address that should be given to the notebook, Mac, or PC during VPN connection setup. It is important to ensure that the IP address is not already used by any device in your home network, so it can not be confused.

Now the assistant can create the configuration files for the FRITZ! Box and the user access. This takes a little while - in the next dialog, you can choose what to do with the created configuration files next.

In order to better understand the settings, the relevant sections of the two created sample files are printed below. In the user-specific configuration file vpnuser.cfg, the dynamic DNS name (here: name.homedns.org) is entered in the target area under name / remotehostname. In addition, the user names (user_fqdn) as well as the encrypted password (key) for establishing the important connection, you always need this information, even if an alternative VPN client is used for access.

The access list specifies the IP network that is allowed to be accessed via VPN. In this case, the remote network has the range 192.168.123.0/24. If necessary, this list can be extended with a comma separated - but this is usually not necessary. If you want to restrict access to a single file server, you can do so here as well - instead of the network you can also enter a single host address.

Remote_virtualip specifies the IP address assigned to the client after the VPN security parameters have been processed. Anyone wishing to subsequently change the IP address will adapt this entry and import the configuration file fritzbox.cfg into the FRITZ! Box again to notify the change.

Import VPN Configuration Into FRITZ! Box

The FRITZ! Box allows up to five simultaneous VPN connections - each one may require its own configuration file. To import the generated configuration file fritzbox.cfg into the FRITZ! Box, first open the user interface of the FRITZ! Box via the web browser. There you can change to Settings /Internet /Remote Access /VPN. The Browse button first selects the corresponding fritzbox.cfg configuration file.

The configuration files for the VPN connection are in Windows 8, Windows 7 and Vista in the directory

% USERPROFILE% \ AppData \ Roaming \ AVM \ FRITZ! VPN \

in Windows XP in the directory

% USERPROFILE% \ Application Data \ AVM \ FRITZ! VPN \

There is a directory with the same name as your dynamic DNS domain name. In it, you will find the configuration file fritzbox.cfg for the FRITZ! Box.

In the next step, access must be set up by the remote user. For Windows users, AVM provides a special client for this, which is installed as described in the next section and set up using the configuration file.

Secure Access To The Home Network With Mac OS X

All you need in addition to the appropriately configured DSL / WLAN router with VPN functionality is a VPN client for Mac OS X, which is available for free. Based on the widespread FRITZ! Box 7170, this practical application case is described here. Depending on the DSL / WLAN router model with VPN functions, it can also be transferred to other models.

If the FRITZ! Box is equipped with the appropriate configuration file; you can also access the home network with a remote Mac. All you need is a VPN client like IPSecuritas (www.lobotomo.com/products/IPSecuritas/index.html). Unlike other commercial solutions, IPSecuritas is freeware and is available for free download.

Start the configuration via Finder / Programs / IPSecuritas and then select connections in the menu bar. Then the following dialog appears:

In the tab General, you enter the dynamic DNS name under Firewall address under which your home network can be reached on the Internet. If you have got a fixed IP address from your internet provider instead, use it. Then enter the IP address you want the Mac to use as a local IP address on the home network in host mode.

In this example, the IP address 192.168.123.201 has been set up. This is located in the same address range as the remote home network, which in this case has been configured under Remote Endpoint /Network with the address range 192.168.123.0 and the network mask / 24 - which corresponds to 255.255.255.0. Then change to the Phase 1 tab.

Otherwise, set the Diffie-Hellman entry in the DH group to 1024 (2), the encryption to AES 256, and the authentication to the hash algorithm SHA-1. For IKE phase 1 mode, set Exchange Mode to Aggressive, see the figure for the other settings.

For local identification, set the option field to USER_FQDN and enter the user ID (here: e-mail address) in the next field. For Remote ID, set Address. Before copying the password from fritzbox.cfg to Preshared Key via copy-and-paste, make sure that the authentication method is set to Preshared Key.

After completing the configuration, close the connection window.

VPN Connection Setup And Data Exchange

The created connection is in the status window of IPSecuritas. If you have now established an internet connection externally, simply start the VPN connection to your home network at home by clicking on the Start button.

After a short moment, the connection is established in the home network. Now the home network shares are available in the Finder.

On the other side - in the home network - the configuration page of the FRITZ! Box also indicates an active incoming VPN connection. In the overview dialog, the green light lights up for remote access.

With an active VPN connection, you can access the available file shares on the home network, such as the NAS server, the Time Capsule network disk, and, of course, the Raspberry Pi. Go here in the Finder menu Go to the dialog Connect to Server. There, you enter the protocol used and the IP address of the share.

For example, with the entry smb: //192.168.123.20, access the Windows-dows / Samba shares of the device with the IP address 192.168.123.20. If you want to open the web interface of the Raspberry Pi, use the address of your home network in the web browser - in this case, the private address 192.168.123.47.

Simple and comfortable: you sit on the sofa and discover something interesting on the Internet, which you would like to print out. So far you have sent the corresponding link by e-mail, so on the iPad or iPhone an e-mail account is configured, this e-mail on the computer opened and then sent from there to the printer. In contrast, you can use the Raspberry Pi in the future directly from iOS to send the print job to the printer - without the annoying detour via the computer. Of course, this only works for iOS applications that support print functionality, such as Mail, Photo, Safari, and more.

Raspberry Pi As An AirPrint Server In The Home Network

To make the Raspberry Pi available as an AirPrint server in the home network for iPhone, iPod touch, or iPad, some dislocations and adjustments are necessary - even when it comes to new iDevices with iOS 6 and the Raspberry Pi in operation. Since this AirPrint function was originally the purchase reason for the Raspberry Pi, this project is still talking about the Debian / Raspian version 6 - Squeezy - which is still available as a download, but now from Debian / Raspian Version 7 - Wheezy - was replaced.

Undocumented: Retrofit AirPrint

If you just want to print something quickly from the iPad or iPhone, the first push comes up against limitations: While a computer simply installs the appropriate driver, this option is not provided for an iOS device such as iPad or iPhone in terms of architecture. Even with the USB cable, you will not get far when connecting to a printer - if you have a wireless network at home, you better use wireless printing over Wi-Fi.

Since 2011, with the update of iOS 4.2.1 for iPhone and iPad, the local printer can be used directly from the hand-flatterer with the AirPrint function in the local network. However, in contrast to the original release version, the printing function has been re-cut from version iOS 5 and the new iPad and works according to the will of Apple initially only on special AirPrint printers from Canon, HP, and others.

To use AirPrint on the official way, there is no need for further installation on iPad or printer. Here you simply use the forwarding function on the iPhone or iPad and select by tap on Print the printer menu. In the next step, the device scans the home Wi-Fi network for AirPrint-compatible printers and lists them in the printer selection. Then send the print job from the iPhone or iPad via WLAN directly to the found printer.

AirPrint Printers by Apple's Grace

The special feature of a so-called AirPrint printer is that it has already integrated the necessary network print server services - here you do not need an intermediary computer, which translates, so to speak, the printout for the printer in printer language. However, with a trick, it is possible to operate a computer-connected printer as an AirPrint printer on the network - then the client computer takes care of the preparation and control of the printer.

An annoying prerequisite for this, however, is that the computer must be switched on permanently - this is depending on the computer used in terms of electricity costs an expensive fun and only in cases really recommended if the computer is already turned on. However, for the provision of a 24/7 service, the Raspberry Pi is the much better choice - and cheaper anyway.

If you do not have a printer with AirPrint function at home, you should - if it goes to Apple - make room in the study and buy a compatible printer. But anyone who already owns a printer (without the AirPrint feature) should look for a more recent firmware version from their printer manufacturer. For example, HP is constantly expanding its AirPrint-compatible printer palette, and some older printers are getting the AirPrint feature later with a firmware update. If a new firmware version is available, install it according to the manufacturer's instructions.

But in times of paperless office, many print on the home computer nothing more or only rarely enough that the printing function on the iPad will probably be used even less frequently. Therefore, the new creation of a printer just because of the AirPrint function makes no sense - here you use the Raspberry Pi and equip it with the Linux printing system CUPS, so as to provide AirPrint functions for free.

Retrofitting AirPrint Printer With Raspberry Pi

Note that once the installation is complete, a 2 GB memory card is almost full - installing printer drivers, PDF features, and the like takes up some space. If the memory card is already getting tight, you should switch to a 4 GB memory card or larger at the latest. First, bring the Raspberry Pi up to date.

If there are too many packages to be updated, the update mechanism sometimes gets out of step and does not find the requested packages right away.

If errors occur, it helps in practice to then trigger the command via console again as a precaution. In the next step, update the installed distribution on the Raspberry Pi with the following command:

sudo apt-get upgrade

In this example, 59 packages had to be updated. Fortunately, the update mechanism tells you how much space is needed.

If there is a lot of space on the SD memory card, you should pay attention to which packages require how much space. Although Debian shares the amount of disk space the packages need to install, it does not mention that there is still room for general work and for the swap file. Side effect: Especially when you have to cope with capacity problems, this also affects the performance - the Raspberry Pi slows down.

The advantage of a freshly updated system is that you avoid any mistakes in advance. Checking for possible dependencies keeps packages reasonably up-to-date, even if they are not explicitly selected for updating.

Of course, not install update and apt-get install upgrade. If you want to operate the Raspberry Pi exclusively as an AirPrint printer and, for example, as a Samba server in the home network, you do not need things such as the graphical desktop and associated tools. Remove them - this creates space on the SD card.

Download And Install CUPS And AirPrint Features

Whether AirPrint function or not - for the use of a printer under Linux, the Common Unix Printing System (CUPS) has prevailed. Here, the printing process is divided into a print client, which sorts and forwards the print jobs, and the print server, which handles the actual printing. These include the classic

CUPS packages such as cups cups-pdf cups-driver-gutenprint also include those for coupling the hardware to provide the classic drivers.

With the large number of available and supported printers, a corresponding number of drivers are installed on the Raspberry Pi. For the AirPrint functionality later programs and services come into play, which in turn access the CUPS functions and thus control the printer. But more on that later, install CUPS from the command line with the following commands:

sudo bash

apt-get install foomatic-db foomatic-db-engine foomatic-filters

apt-get install cups cups-pdf cups-driver-goodprint

gutenprint has nothing to do with a former Defense Minister of the Federal Republic of Germany, but is a driver collection of printer manufacturers such as Canon, Epson, Lexmark, Sony, Olympus and PCL printers, which can be used after installation with Ghostscript, CUPS, Foomatic and GIMP.

If the memory card is too tight, it may make sense to check first whether the printer used is supported by gutenprint or not. In the latter case you could do without sprint print if you can get a suitable CUPS driver for your printer from the manufacturer for Debian 6.

If the storage space does not play a major role, the installation makes sense, not least for reasons of compatibility. Even if you later want to retrofit a printer, the printer may be ready for use immediately.

Owners of a Hewlett-Packard printer must install the hplip package:

sudo apt-get install hplip

sudo apt-get install pycups python2 python-cups

Then, if not already installed, install the Python scripting language and the pycups or python-cups connector, which is responsible for using the CUPS 1.2 API in Python programs, allowing Python-based programs to print.

Now the Linux printing system CUPS with printer should be installed. Now download and configure the Avahi driver or daemon, which provides the actual AirPrint functionality. If you have already installed the hplip package in the case of an HP printer, avahi and mDNS are usually already on board. In spite of this, you play it safe again and reinstall the package in case of doubt.

Mandatory: Install Avahi and mDNS server

For the actual AirPrint function you need besides CUPS still further packages, which are to be installed only after the successful CUPS installation. With the following command you get the basic packages, which in turn check their dependencies and, if necessary, reload further packages until the actual program is installed properly.

sudo apt-get install avahi avahi-daemon avahi-discover libnss-mdns

Only with the installation of avahi and libnss-mdns you make sure that the CUPS Raspberry can also perform its Bonjour function for the iOS devices in the home network. In addition to mDNS (Multicast DNS) Bonjour uses DNS Service Discovery (DNS-SD). After installation, the mDNS responder is automatically set up on the Raspberry, which answers the query and reply requests of the iOS devices.

With Tildesoft's Discovery Browser (available for free from the iTunes Store), you can use your iPhone or iPad to test the Bonjour capabilities of the Raspberry Pi installation - scanning the entire home network for Bonjour-enabled devices, so to speak.

In principle, when using CUPS, you also need an administrative user who can not only install the printer, but can also later make various settings for maintenance purposes via the CUPS configuration page. Basically, this user must also have a user account on the appropriate machine - in this case, the Raspberry Pi -; just use the existing user pi - in this example with the default password raspberry. This user must be added to the appropriate CUPS group - the lpadmin group - using the usermod command from the command line.

sudo usermod -ag lpadmin pi

If you have already set up a different username for this purpose, use it for this purpose. In the example below, we create a user named printer and password printerpassword.

sudo adduser printer

sudo usermod -ag lpadmin printer

If the user is created and a member of the lpadmin group, start CUPS for the first time in the default configuration. The installation and configuration of the actual printer or the adjustment for AirPrint will be done in the next step. First of all, it's about fixing the CUPS printing system as the basis for the next steps.

To do this, start CUPS and then start the Avahi daemon via the command line:

sudo /etc/init.d/cups start

sudo /etc/init.d/avahi-daemon start

If errors occur at the start of the two services, you must re-install the packages as described above - both are essential for the next steps.

If the CUPS daemon is running, you can log in to the CUPS configuration page for the first time - but before doing so, you must first set the appropriate port and enable access for local clients to CUPS.

All At Home? - Configure Access To CUPS

The first port of call for CUPS configuration on the command line is the cupsd.conf file located in the / etc / cups directory. Here is an overview of the most important changes for the AirPrint access - you will find out in detail later which interventions are necessary.

Server Alias *

Port 631

Lists /var/run/cups/cups.sock

To implement the required changes for CUPS, open the CUPS configuration file with the command

sudo nano /etc/cups/cupsd.conf

Depending on the editor used (here: nano), first navigate downwards with the arrow keys until you reach the entry localhost: 631. Here, CUPS listens for jobs on the local machine (localhost) at port 631.

That's a good idea, but we want to use the printer from the entire home network, so CUPS should listen not only to localhost but basically to port 631.

For this reason, the entry localhost: 631 is commented out by a preceding picket symbol (#), and in the following line the entry port 631 is set. These changes were made with Change1-Airprint and Change2-Airprint documented.

So that the CUPS printer is visible for each device in the home network and no longer deals too sensitively with inquiries, which do not bring a correct HTTP header, the basic access for all (*) is allowed - thus also for Apple's Bonjour services or devices who use this technique.

To do this, enter the parameter ServerAlias * in cupsd.conf, if possible at the beginning. This change is documented in the figure with Change3-Airprint, the remaining three (Change4-Airprint, Change5-Airprint, Change6-Airprint) concern the access to the corresponding configuration pages on the CUPS web frontend, the admin page and the configuration files. The parameter Allow @LOCAL was set here for access. For example, if you want to restrict access to the configuration pages, it is best to use the @SYSTEM switch, which ensures that only members of the lpadmin system group can access them.

<Location / admin / conf>
AuthType Basic
Require user @SYSTEM
Order allow, deny
</ Location>

If you now want to allow access to the system from the network, this is done as in our example by Allow @LOCAL - which ensures that all computers (and the iPhones, iPads, etc.) in the local network access the corresponding CUPS service allowed. The @LOCAL parameter is nothing more than the IP address range in which the CUPS server is operated. Once the desired changes have been made, save the file by pressing [Ctrl] + [X] together with the overwrite confirmation.

sudo /etc/init.d/cups restart

Then restart the CUPS service on the Raspberry Pi to enable the changes you have made and then log in to the CUPS administration page.

Use Admin Website: Pair Printer With CUPS

CUPS has a built-in web server, accessible via port 631, which is used to set up and manage the printers. Naturally, the CUPS admin page can be reached at the same IP address as the Raspberry Pi. Anyone who does not operate a DNS server in the home network or has simply forgotten this IP address will get it on the console of the Raspberry Pi via ifconfig command. In this example, the Raspberry Pi can be reached via 192.168.123.28 - port 631 has been set in the configuration file. In effect, this means that by entering 192.168.123.28:631 in the address bar of the web browser from any computer on your home network, you will reach the CUPS summary page on the Raspberry Pi.

Now navigate to the Administration tab and release the printer to be added. Basically, it is the case with the admin page that every user is allowed to perform all actions here - if you would like to add a printer, a password prompt appears when changing. For this, you previously specified an appropriate username during setup, which is also a member of the Linux group lpadmin on the Raspberry Pi. In this example, there was the Raspberry Pi user pi and the newly created user named printer, which was also added to the lpadmin group.

Check the box when releasing printers connected to this system and click the Change settings button to apply. Afterwards, the website expects a renewed confirmation of the change. Do not be intimidated by the possibly appearing page. The security certificate of the website is untrustworthy - at the IP address you can see that this is your print server. Therefore, click the Next / Continue button on this page.

Now that you have authenticated yourself to CUPS, you can set up the CUPS printer (s) available on your home network configuration page.

Adding And Setting Up Printers In The Home Network To CUPS

Ingenious - if you have a printer with a USB interface, you can now plug it into the Raspberry Pi and switch it on. Thanks to the Raspberry Pi, you have a cost-effective print server in the home network, which you can now use from all computers at home. In addition to the printers that can be connected to the Raspberry Pi, CUPS naturally also supports printers that are located on other computers in the home network (and released there), as well as the classic network printers that come with a built-in print server and also an IP address in the home network are reachable.

No matter which printer or printer type you use - local printers connected directly to the Raspberry Pi, network-accessible printers, and printers on remote print servers are set up using the same steps in CUPS. It is only important that the printer (s) are turned on and can be reached directly or indirectly via the home network.

Start by searching the home network for available printers.

Clicking the List Available Printers button already has many devices found automatically.

Now click on the Next button and select the driver of the found printer, which should normally already be included in the CUPS package. After a few moments, a whole range of available drivers will appear.

Many drivers are often listed for a model - which of them provides the best print quality and performance is perhaps an experience you need to classify yourself. Now the printer is added to the CUPS configuration, but does it print as well? You can start the test print in the tab Printer with the respective printer via the pop-up field Maintenance with the option Print Test Page.

If a test page emerges from the connected printer in just a few minutes, you have successfully set up CUPS.

For example, to put the configured CUPS printer of the Raspberry Pi in the home network for the computers in operation, there the installation of a network printer is necessary. For example, in Windows, select Printers from the Control Panel and click the Add Printer option in the menu area to start the Add Printer Wizard.

In addition to a normal, local printer, the Add a network, wireless or Bluetooth printer option is also available. Click on the Windows network shares of the connected PCs to see the shares or shared printers.

Alternatively, you can also click on the option The printer you are looking for is not listed and select the shared printer manually by browsing. Choose these now. In the dialog that opens, enter the address of the Raspberry Pi / CUPS server in the Select shared printer name box:

http: // <IP address-Raspberry>: 631 / printers / <printer name-with-CUPS configuration>

In this example we use

http://192.168.123.28:631/printers/HP_LaserJet_2100_Series

After clicking Next, Windows is now looking for available drivers - and the Raspberry Pi: Here, the installation mechanism connects and offers the appropriate drivers to choose from. In this case, first select the manufacturer and then in the right window under Printer the appropriate printer model.

Subsequently, if desired, the name of the printer name can be adapted.

If CUPS has activated the corresponding drivers for the network printer, click on Next. In the next step, the printer installation assistant with a summary dialog in which you can initiate the printing of a test page.

The next step is to pair CUPS with the AirPrint peer - the Avahi Daemon - that keeps the network up to date on iOS devices.

Automatic AirPrint Installation With Python Script

In order for the changes made to remain even after a restart of the Raspberry Pi, you still need support. For this purpose, it is necessary to include a suitable script (https://github.com/tjfontaine/airprint-generate), which automatically performs this task. Here's the easiest way to bend the Raspberry Pi so that this script works the way it should - unless you're proficient in the Python scripting language. First create the necessary directory / opt / airprint and change to the directory via cd command.

sudo mkdir / opt / airprint

cd / opt / airprint

sudo wget -O airprint-generate.py - no-check-certificate https://raw.github.com/tjfontaine/airprint-generate/master/airprint-generate.py

sudo chmod 755 airprint-generate.py

Then load the script per wget directly from the author of the Python script (Timothy Fontaine) to the Raspberry Pi. Note that the above sudo wget command spans two lines. After a moment, you downloaded the 10K script.

Then set the access permissions of the Python script with the command

sudo chmod 755 airprint-generate.py

This allows the owner of the file to write, read and execute, while the group and all others are allowed to read and execute. That is completely sufficient.

Password Protection When Printing

If a user and a password are required for printing under CUPS, these must also be specified in the Python script. To do this, open the file in an editor and search for the string # air = username, password, which you comment out and then populate with the user and the corresponding password.

In our case everyone in the household is allowed to use the CUPS printer, no CUPS access protection has been activated. The next step is to generate the necessary service file for AirPrint using the downloaded Python script. The goal is here

/ Etc / avahi / services.

sudo ./airprint-generate.py -d / etc / avahi / services

Now the Python script recreates the services file and writes it to the / etc / avahi / services directory, which is completed after a moment.

iOS 6 In Action? - Retrofit AirPrint To Raspberry Pi

The previously introduced solution works smoothly for iOS 5 devices. However, since the release of iOS 6 in the fall of 2012, many of the printers have stopped appearing after the iOS 6 update, or access to the printer has run out of space. After the release of iOS 6, it was not long before the complaints in the Apple forums under apple.com up under the blanket, because Apple has again cut the AirPrint support as at the time when switching from iOS 4 to i OS 5. Here's where customization of two configuration files helps to get the CUPS printing system back on track for AirPrint.

Never change a running system: As a precaution, you should make a backup of the files to be processed, so that you can easily restore the original state if necessary.

ls / etc / avahi / services

First check the services file for the created AirPrint printer and, if necessary, save the original with the cp command. After opening the file, this shows the following contents:

<? xml version = "1.0"?> <! DOCTYPE service-group SYSTEM 'avahi-
service.dtd '> <service-group> <name replace-wildcards = "yes"> AirPrint
HP_LaserJet_2100_Series @
% H </ name> <service> <type> _ipp._tcp </ type> <subtype> _universal._sub._ipp._tcp </ subtype> <port> 631 </ port> <txt record> txtvers = 1 </ txt record> <txt
record> Q total = 1 </ txt record> <txt record> Transparent = T </ txt record> <txt
record> URF = none </ txt record> <txt
record> rp = printers / HP_LaserJet_2100_Series </ txt record> <txt record> note = HP
LaserJet 2100 Series </ txt-record> <txt-record> product = (GPL Ghostscript) </ txt
record> <txt record> printer-state = 3 </ txt record> <txt record> PRINTER
type = 0x80901c </ txt record> <txt record> pdl = application / octet
stream, application / pdf, application / postscript, image / gif, image / jpeg, image / png,
Image / tiff, text / html, text / plain, application / openofficeps, application / vnd.cu
ps banner, application / vnd.cups-pdf, application / vnd.cups-postscript </ txt

record> </ service> </ service group>

Here the expression image / urf is missing at the end of the line:

pdl = application / octet

stream, application / pdf, application / postscript, image / gif, image / jpeg, image / png,

Image / tiff, text / html, text / plain, application / openofficeps, application / vnd.cu

ps banner, application / vnd.cups-pdf, application / vnd.cups-postscript, image / urf

However, this control is not mandatory and certainly not necessary, as this file is automatically rebuilt when the airprint-generate.py script is restarted. After all, according to the facts available, a change to two files is necessary. First, back up this by cp command:

sudo cp /usr/share/cups/mime/mime.types /usr/share/cups/mime/mime.types.org sudo cp /usr/share/cups/mime/mime.convs/usr/share/ cups / mime /mime.convs.org

Then open the mime.types configuration file, which will make the CUPS printer appear as a device on the iOS device.

sudo nano /usr/share/cups/mime/mime.types

There you add the line

image / original (0, UNIRAST)

into the file - pay attention to the distances that you create with the [Tab] key.

The same applies to the file mime.convs.

sudo nano /usr/share/cups/mime/mime.convs

There you add the line

image / urf application / vnd.cups-postscript 66 pdftops

also clean with intervals by [Tab] key in the configuration file. Once the changes have been saved, change to the directory / opt / airprint /:

cd / opt / airprint /
sudo ./airprint-generate.py -d / etc / avahi / services
and restart the AirPrint Python script. This rewrites the services file and saves it for the printer in the / etc / avahi / services directory, which is completed after a short while. Then start with the command
sudo /etc/init.d/avahi-daemon restart
Re-activate the Bonjour service on the Raspberry Pi to enable the changes made.
AirPrint HP_LaserJet_2100_Series @ raspi-airprint._ipp._tcp.local. IPP (Internet Printing Protocol)
Raspi-airprint.local: 631
192.168.123.28:631
note = HP LaserJet 2100 series
pdl = application / octet
stream, application / pdf, application / postscript, image / gif, image / jpeg, image / png,
Image / tiff, text / html, text / plain, application / openofficeps, application / vnd.cu
ps banner, application / vnd.cups-pdf, application / vnd.cups-postscript, image / urf
printer-state = 3
printer-type = 0x80901c
product = (GPL Ghostscript)
qtotal = 1
rp = printers / HP_LaserJet_2100_Series
Transparent = T
txt = 1
URF = none
If you use the Tildesoft Discoverer on your iPad or iPhone, you will receive an output when parsing the IPP (Internet Printing Protocol), in which you will now also find the required image / urf parameter.

When using AirPrint, certain functions, such as duplex printing, selecting a different paper tray, etc. may not be available.

In the menu Print ...
Select a printer ...
print options
choose ...
The print job has been issued.

After a short moment, the connected printer will go off. Now, thanks to the Raspberry Pi, you are fully equipped in your home network - in addition to the computers, thanks to the retrofitted Bonjour function, you now also print with the iDevices from Cupertino.

With Apple's AirPlay technology, content from the iOS, such as iPhone or iPad, can simply be streamed wirelessly to the connected speakers via Raspberry Pi. The only thing you need is a wireless LAN network, speakers, and a Raspberry Pi that you can set up as an AirPlay device in minutes. Of course, you can also use the installed on the Raspberry Pi solution from a computer in the home network on which iTunes is located - but come iTunes and the iPhone or iPad from the same home.

Jack As Standard Output Device For Audio

Normally, the audio output of the Raspberry Pi is active by default. If you want to be on the safe side, the 3.5 mm jack output is fixed as a standard audio output device. To do this, use the command on the command line:

amixer cset numid = 3 1

In this case, the value 1 is in the command for the 3.5 mm headphone jack output - basically you can assign this value as follows:

Outputs value
Automatic 0
3.5mm headphone jack output 1
Audio over HDMI 2

If an error occurs (amixer: command not found), this is because in this case the audio support is not (yet) installed or has been uninstalled.

sudo bash
apt-get install alsa-utils
modprobe snd_bcm2835

Anyway - for AirPlay you need of course the audio output of the Raspberry Pi, so that the connected speakers can also be filled with music.

Then insert the driver into the system via modprobe and activate it. Then restart the configuration of the default output device for audio playback:

amixer cset numid = 3 1

In the next step, the Raspberry Pi preparations are done, now you can install the free Shairport package and put into operation.

Installing Shairport Package

First, bring the Raspberry Pi up to date and then install various packages necessary for the successful completion of the installation. Although git and perl are usually found on the Raspberry Pi - here you can get the installation for safety's sake:

sudo apt-get update
sudo apt-get install git libao-dev libssl-dev libcrypt-openssl-rsa-perl libio-socket-inet6-perl libwww-perl avahi-utils pkg-config

When you're ready to install Shairport, clone github.com's Shairport repository to the pi user's local / home directory on the Raspberry Pi.

sudo git clone https://github.com/albertz/shairport.git shairport cd ~ / shairport
sudo make && make install
sudo apt-get install pkg-config
sudo make && make install

If errors occur again, perform the installation with full root privileges.
Execute the make and then the make install command for the installation.
To do this, open a root console with sudo bash, clean up again and start the
Compile again:
sudo bash
make clean
make && make install

This process takes another few minutes.
Before you configure Shairport to your environment and start it automatically after booting the Raspberry Pi, install a Session Description Protocol (SDP) bug fix file that will allow iOS 6 devices to run successfully Shairport is necessary:
wget http://www.inf.udec.cl/~diegocaro/talleracm/libnet-sdp-perl_0.07-1_all.deb
sudo dpkg -i libnet-sdp-perl_0.07-1_all.deb

After installing the libnet-sdp-perl_0.07-1_all.deb file via dpkg -i, the installed shairport has now been updated to the latest iPad and iPod support. Now configure Shairport for the automatic start, if the Raspberry Pi is restarted.

Setting Up Shairport

In the created source directory of Shairport is a sample file, which you also need as a startup file with a small adjustment for the Raspberry Pi. These are copied to the start directory

/etc/init.d/ of the Raspberry Pi, where all startup scripts are located, and set the appropriate permissions of the file, so that it can also be executed at system startup.

sudo bash
cd /etc/init.d
cp ~ / shairport / shairport.init.sample /etc/init.d/shairport
chmod a + x shairport
update-rc.d shairport defaults
insserv shairport

In the next step, change the daemon start arguments to a name that the iPhone or iPad should later use to find the Raspberry Pi.

sudo nano shairport

To do this, customize the startup file /etc/init.d/shairport and change the entry DAEMON_ARGS there. This is originally:

DAEMON_ARGS = "- w $ PIDFILE"

Here you comment out the old entry by picket symbol and add the new one

Line on:

DAEMON_ARGS = "- w $ PIDFILE -a rAirPort"

Alternatively, you can of course directly change the corresponding line of code in the script, which is up to you.

After saving the file and quitting the editor, for safety's sake restart the shairport service on the Raspberry Pi.

sudo /etc/init.d/shairport restart

In the next step, you can connect the speakers to the Raspberry Pi and pick up the iPad or iPhone from which you want to stream music to the Raspberry Pi.

Using Shairport On The iPhone

Start as usual the music app on the iPhone and navigate to your favorite music playlist. Start any song on the iPhone - now the song should be heard through the built-in speakers of the iPhone. To redirect the audio output to the speakers connected to the Raspberry Pi, select the AirPlay icon.

If the Raspberry Pi is not visible as a speaker, start the iPhone on the iPhone Settings dialog and check if you are also in the same network as the Raspberry Pi - if necessary, deactivating and activating the network settings. Simply switch to flight mode and exit again - then the Raspberry Pi will be available as an AirPlay device.

Uses: Webcam and Raspberry Pi

If you have a zero-fifteen webcam - like a Playstation 3 - lying around, you can use the Raspberry Pi to bring it back to life and use it as a webcam, for example. Since this combination not only works, but is also economically recommendable in times of high electricity prices due to the low power consumption of the Raspberry Pi, the presented solution is all the more attractive.

Here you first install the known under Linux FFMpeg package, which is responsible for the compression of the captured images and makes them available for other applications, such as for web page transmission in a media player-capable format as MJPEG stream or simple for a remote media player like VLC on another computer.

Obtain And Compile FFMpeg

The widespread FFMpeg package is unfortunately not included in the standard package sources of the Raspberry Pi and must be added manually. Then you need to download and compile the package for the Raspberry Pi. But one by one - first add the reference source for FFMpeg to the Raspberry Pi configuration.

Edit Sources

In order to edit the package sources on the Debian-Wheezy-Raspberry, you need to have administrative privileges, which you get from the leading sudo:
sudo nano /etc/apt/sources.list
Here you add the two lines
deb-src http://www.deb-multimedia.org sid main
deb http://www.deb-multimedia.org wheezy main non-free
just add to the already existing ones.
To initialize the new sources and put them into operation, you now have one
Update with the following command through:
sudo apt-get update
Initialize sources and adjust again
Then install the deb-multimedia package from the "new" source.
keyring:
sudo apt-get install deb-multimedia-keyring nano /etc/apt/sources.list
Once done, edit the package source configuration file again and comment the line deb http://www.deb-multimedia.org wheezy main non-free using the leading picket fence icon or delete the line completely from the File /etc/apt/sources.list.
The next step is to load the sources from the actual FFMpeg package.

Get And Compile FFMpeg Source Files

Tailor-made compiling is boring and time-consuming for the perfect adaptation to the target system, but it has the advantage that the finished solution usually works as well. First, get the sources via apt-get command:
sudo apt-get source ffmpeg-dmo
Switch to the source directory with the cd command. It's best to use the autocomplete function of the [Tab] key - this helps a lot to get you to the right destination directory.

cd ffmpeg-dmo-0.11
./configure
make && make install

With the start of the script ./configure you trigger the compilation and configuration of the existing source files, in order to then install them on the Raspberry via make or make install.

Then the FFMpeg package is ready for use on the Raspberry Pi.

Stream Audio

If you also want to transfer audio data - ie sounds - via the connected webcam during streaming, this must of course support the webcam, ie have a built-in microphone. In addition, the ALSA sound package must be installed on the Raspberry Pi.

Sound Desired? - Switch on ALSA

To do this, open the configuration file for the package sources with the nano-editor:

sudo nano /etc/apt/sources.list

and add two package sources:

deb-src http://www.deb-multimedia.org sid main
deb http://www.deb-multimedia.org wheezy main non-free

After initializing the package sources with

apt-get update

Now install the sound support after:

apt-get install deb-multimedia-keyring libasound2-dev

Then a reworking of the repositories is required - as is known, the line must

deb http://www.deb-multimedia.org wheezy main non-free

in the package file

/etc/apt/sources.list

be deleted or commented out. If not available, download the Sources of FFMpeg again on the Raspberry Pi:

apt-get source ffmpeg-dmo
go to the directory and lead with
./configure
such as make && make install
Compile and create the FFMpegs package again - this time with sound support. In the next step, you can configure FFMpeg and put it into operation.
The operation of a service or program usually requires parameters that are created in a configuration file belonging to the package. In this case, you create such a file in the / etc directory using the touch command itself:
sudo touch / etc / ffmpegserver.conf
To fill the created file with content, open it with the nano-Editor:
sudo nano /etc/ffmpegserver.conf
and add the following lines there:
Port 80
BindAddress 0.0.0.0
MaxClients 5
MaxBandwidth 50000
nodaemon
<Feed picam.ffm>
file /tmp/picam.ffm
FileMaxSize 10M
</ Feed>
<Stream picam.mjpeg>
Feed picam.ffm
Format mjpeg
Video Size 640x480
VideoFrameRate 10
VideoBitRate 2000
VideoQMin 1
VideoQMax 9

</ Stream>

The entries are self-explanatory. If you want to run the webcam on a port other than the default Web server port 80, change this value. The limitation on the number of concurrent accesses (here: 5) and the maximum bandwidth help to conserve the Raspberry Pi resources. Afterwards, a feed and the stream are created - with the latter you enter with VideoSize the values that your webcam connected to the Raspberry Pi supplies. With a meager network connection, it helps to reduce this value to 320x240. Save this file now.

So that the installed FFMpeg server also knows where its configuration lies and with which parameters or which device it should work with at all, you also create a start script that ensures that the camera runs even after a restart of the Raspberry Pi. With the command

sudo nano /usr/sbin/picam.sh

create the file - in our example we call it picam.sh - in the directory / usr / sbin and carry the configuration there

ffserver -f /etc/ffmpegserver.conf & ffmpeg -v verbose -r 5 -s 640x480 -f video4linux2 -i / dev / video0 http: //localhost/picam.ffm

After registering and saving the file, it must be made executable as usual under Linux. The easiest way to do this is with the command

chmod + x /usr/sbin/picam.sh

Now the preparations are finished, in the next step you can put the Web-cam into operation.

If the created script has execute permissions, start the script with the following command on the command line:

/usr/sbin/picam.sh

Now you can put this stream in a window in your own website or display the generated feed (here: picam.ffm) via a web browser. However, you are more flexible with a network-capable video player such as the VLC, which dominates the playback of network streams from the outset.

Raspberry Pi as Electronic Watchdog: What was a huge expense and effort a couple of years ago is now done with a Raspberry Pi and the purchase of one or two cameras directly or through the home network connected to the Raspberry Pi. Next, set up a system that lets you monitor and record 24/7 events from use as a multimedia baby monitor to house or property monitoring.

However, a permanent recording costs not only computing power, but also storage capacity - a good compromise here is to turn on the camera's motion detection on the Raspberry Pi and start the recording only when it is necessary. Or you only specify specific image areas for which monitoring is to be activated. Anyway, with the Raspberry Pi

Put together a home and property supervision, which is optimally tailored to your needs.

Install Zone Minder Via Apt-Get

For the installation of Zoneminder at least one SD memory card of 4 GB or more is recommended. Since the default image size of the Debian image files is usually adapted to 2 GB memory cards, the memory card must be adapted in accordance with the instructions, thus also providing the necessary space for the Raspberry Pi or the operating system and Zoneminder to provide.

The following sequence of commands is necessary to completely install Zone Zone and its dependent packages and to put them into operation for the first time:

sudo bash

apt-get update

apt-get install zoneminder

service zoneminder restart
service zoneminder status
After installing and starting Zoneminder, restart the Zone-less restart call to see if stopping the dependent services will work properly and restart them. You can then use the status parameter to display the status of Zoneminder on the console.

Pair Zone Children With Apache Web Server

Basically, the Apache web server is always co-installed with the Zoneminder package, even if an alternative web server is already on the Raspberry. However, apart from the system resources, Apache is a good choice for zoeminder operation, since Apache is already well configured and running at the factory. But for automated startup or operation under Apache you have to create a link to the zone minor configuration file and restart Apache to activate the change.

sudo bash
ln -s /etc/zm/apache.conf
/etc/apache2/conf.d/zoneminder.conf
/etc/init.d/apache2 force-reload

If you want to make sure that Apache or Zoneminder really works after a restart of the Raspberry Pi, start with the command

reboot

the Raspberry and then activates the root-
Access to the console:
sudo bash
In the next step you create a system user for zone-minor.

Mandatory: Create users for zone children

In order for Zoneminder to work properly after installation, it is necessary that you create a user for the application on the Raspberry Pi. With the command

sudo adduser www-data video

add the user wwww-data to the group video.

No Firefox? - Install Cambozola

As you know, not all web browsers around the world react the same, from the presentation to the format. Here, the Zoneminder developers recommend the installation of a plug-in - in this case Cambozola, which until then was known to the author only from the cheese counter. Cambozola is a Java-written plug-in that can decode multipart JPEG streams in the browser - for users of the Internet explorer thus necessary. To install Cambozola, do the following for the Raspberry Pi in the terminal:

sudo bash
cd / usr / src
wget http://www.charliemouse.com:8080/code/cambozola/cambozola-latest.tar.gz tar -xzvf cambozola-latest.tar.gz
cp cambozola-0.92 / dist / cambozola.jar / usr / share / zoneminder

First, initialize the root environment and load the latest version of Cambozola via wget command on the Raspberry into the directory / usr / src.
/ Usr / share / zone less directory.
Now restart the zoneminder process via service zoneminder restart:
Afterwards, the zoneminder developers recommend an apt-get update and an apt-get upgrade to update the overall system as well as dependencies on Zoneminder.

Apache Fine Tuning and Bug Fix

Especially when you're on the road, you do not want to remember long domain names. Since the Raspberry with Zoneminder is more than enough busy, Zoneminder can also be used directly as the root directory for the web server, so

that when entering the zone-minor front-end, the entry of the zm-abbreviation in the address is superfluous. Thus, instead of the address http: // <IP-Address / DNS-Name-RaspberryPi> / zm the call of http: // <IP-Address / DNS-Name-RaspberryPi> will suffice. For this open the file 000-default.
sudo bash
nano / etc / apache2 / sites-enabled / 000-default
There replace the entry
DocumentRoot / var / www
With
DocumentRoot / usr / share / zoneminder
such as
<Directory / var / www / >
With
<Directory / usr / share / zoneminder / >
and save the file.
Then restart the webserver. For this you use this command:
service apache2 restart
If the message Could not Reliably Determine the server's fully qualified domain name, using 127.0.1.1 for ServerName, appears after restarting the Raspberry Pi or the Apache daemon on the console, a small break in the configuration file httpd.conf will help:
sudo bash
nano /etc/apache2/httpd.conf
Here you add the entry at the end of the file
ServerName localhost
After a restart of Apache, the error message on the console should now be a thing of the past.
If Zoneminder is properly installed, the webcam models connected to the Raspberry Pi can only be used if they are naturally also supported by Debian Linux itself. If a camera is

plugged into the Raspberry Pi via USB, first check with the dmesg command on the console if the camera was even recognized by the system. If so, see if the camera is also available as a so-called device link in the Raspberry Pi:

ls / dev / video *

Output:

/ dev / video0 / dev / video1

In this example, both USB ports of the Raspberry are occupied by two identical webcams (PS3 Eye camera, under 10 Euro each). If you change devices or one is not active, you will be forced to change the zoneminder configuration accordingly, as the associated / dev / video0 source is now different.

Remedy is the use of the fixed device links, which hide in / dev / v4l / by-id and / dev / v4l / by-path - here, however, there is the problem that Zoneminder does not support too long path information in the source field. Therefore, Zoneminder truncates the specified path, which by its nature can not be found.

ls / dev / v4l / by-path /

Output:

platform-bcm2708_usb-usb-0:   1.2:   1.0-video-index0
platform-bcm2708_usb-usb-0: 1.3: 1.0-video-index0

Since this device path is definitely too long for zone children, the detour helps with a symbolic link for each individual camera, which can then also be used for zone children.

sudo bash

cd /

mkdir / cam

chmod 777 / cam

cd / cam

Then create a symbolic link to the corresponding device file in this directory for the connected camera:

Here you can use a separate directory for each connected camera. With the ln command, left the directory of / cam / c1 on the long path /dev/v4l/by-path/platform-bcm2708_usb-usb-0:1.2:1.0-video-index0:

ln   /dev/v4l/by-path/platform-bcm2708_usb-usb-0:1.2:1.0-video-index0 c1

Now the result of the trick can also be used in Zoneminder. Now start the web browser on the computer.

To access the web frontend of Zoneminder, simply enter the IP address of the Raspberry Pi in the address bar of the web browser. By default, Zoneminder is configured so that you can access all areas of Zoneminder without additional authentication. By default, the zone minor installation is over which IP address the Raspberry Pi uses can be found in the console via ifconfig-Command. In this example, the Raspberry Pi uses the IP address 192.168.123.47:

http://192.168.123.47/zm

If you have run the Apache hack from the section "Apache fine-tuning and bug-fixes" and use Zoneminder directly as the root directory for the web server, the zm shortcut in the address is superfluous. In this case, just use the address

http://192.168.123.47

to get to the Zoneminder overview page.

Here are some more small work to do before you get to see the video image of the webcam for the first time. First, add a new monitor (Add New Monitor button). In this new dialog box, first enter a meaningful name for the monitor in Name.

In the Source tab, first enter the created device path (in this example, the symbolic link / cam / c1) and select the Capture Method Video For Linux version 2 entry. For the camera (here: PS3 Eye) are the device format PAL and the color palette YUYV registered.

320 or 240 pixels are used for the resolution - here, the PS3 Eye camera is already at the limit. For the camera-specific values in this dialog you will find the right parameters for many models in the Zoneminder Wiki (http://www.zoneminder.com/wiki/).

If you do not already have a webcam and need a camera for the Raspberry, you will also find information about whether the model you are looking for works with Zoneminder.

If you want to connect more than one webcam to the Raspberry Pi and use it with Zoneminder, add the second webcam to the Zoneminder configuration as described above. Although technically feasible, an active USB hub can also connect multiple USB cameras (up to four) to the Raspberry, but the system performance of the Raspberry Pi and Zoneminder operation will suffer significantly. After entering and configuring the monitors, they now appear in the Zoneminder overview page - the link Montage is now also visible.

If Zoneminder is configured, the monitor does not have to be in operation, and an image can be seen on the assembly website. But even if a picture is transmitted immediately and is visible, it is advisable to initially view the log file - for reasons of the limited system resources of the Raspberry Pi.

Fix The Webcam Bug Of Zoneminder

To see the log file or the running content, simply click on the log link in the upper right area of Zoneminder to follow the system messages of Zoneminder. In this case, the recurring shared data size conflict error is immediately noticeable.

To fix this error, open the Memory.pm file that is responsible for Zoneminder's storage management with an editor of your choice - nano in this example -:

sudo bash
nano /usr/local/share/perl/5.12.4/ZoneMinder/Memory.pm

If the file is open, look for the section
$ arch = int (3.2 * length (~ 0));
and replace it with
$ arch = 32;
The most convenient option is to uncomment the entry (erroneous for the Raspberry Pi) with a picket fence symbol # and set the arch variable to the new value on the next line.
In the next step you start Zoneminder by command
service zoneminder restart
and then check the zoneminder log file.
To view the log file again, click on the log link of Zone-minder again.
Every entry in the log file - ie writing the log files with everything else - draws system resources, and these are known to be rare on the Raspberry Pi. Here you should eliminate all visible error messages, and then later think about switching off the writing of the log file in the options of Zoneminder.

Eliminate Lib-JPEG Error Message

Anyone connecting a so-called IP camera to the Raspberry in addition to a webcam connected locally to the Raspberry Pi may also come into contact with another phenomenon in the log file: Another recurring error message in the log indicates a problem in the JPEG library, but in practice - in the console - the transferred files are fine. Another reason to eliminate the error message here and to clear the log file of Zoneminder.

In the first step, you get the download link to download the JPEG sources via wget command to the Raspberry Pi. Just look for the filename jpegsrc.v8d.tar.gz on your computer, or use the browser to go to www.ijg.org/files. There is the file or even a more recent version to find - load it now via the console of the Raspberry with the following command in the home directory of the user Pi.

wget http://www.ijg.org/files/ jpegsrc.v8d.tar.gz tar -xzvf jpegsrc.v8d.tar.gz

After unzipping by tar command, navigate to the / home / pi / jpeg-8d directory and open the file jdmarker.c with the nano-Editor:

sudo bash

/ Home / pi / jpeg-8d

nano jdmarker.c

There, use the key combination [Ctrl] + [W] to search for the string if (cinfo-> marker-> discarded_bytes) and comment, as shown in the following illustration, by entering the comment characters / * and * /

WARNMS2 (cinfo, JWRN_EXTRANEOUS_DATA, cinfo-> marker-> discarded_bytes, c);

out.

After changing the source code, create your own version of the custom JPEG package. First, prepare the available sources

./configure

on, then in the next step with

make && make install

to compile the JPEG package.

In the next step, replace the original ones with the newly compiled Lib JPEG files. To gain easy access to the files, do the following: Start a root shell, exit the Zoneminder service, make a backup copy to make any changes you can undo, and copy the two files to their new location:

sudo bash

service zoneminder stop

mv ./usr/arm-linux-gnueabi/lib/libc.so.8 ./usr/arm-linux-gnueabi/lib/libc.so.8.old

mv ./usr/arm-linux-gnueabi/lib/libc.so.8.4.0 ./usr/arm-linux-gnueabi/lib/libc.so.8.4.0.old

cp   ./home/pi/jpeg-8/libc.so.8   ./usr/arm-linux-gnueabi/lib/libc.so.8
cp   ./home/pi/jpeg-8/libc.so.8.4.0   ./usr/arm-linux-gnueabi/lib/libc.so.8.4.0 service zoneminder start

After restarting Zoneminder, the JPEG errors should now be a thing of the past. If you want to upgrade the Raspberry to an apartment / home monitoring center, Zoneminder now has all the options that would go beyond the scope of this book.

Pair IP Camera with Raspberry Pi

Cameras for indoor and outdoor use can be done easily - and these are not even expensive: So can be found in the 50-Euro price range consistently usable models, which in the featured Zoneminder configuration (almost) immediately put into operation can be.

If the budget for the purchase of an IP camera is in the 50 Euro price range, you usually end up with different models of China models, which are generally identical, but from different manufacturers and dealers different platforms such as Amazon, eBay etc.

Thus, the manufacturers EasyN, Foscam and Wansview with the same camera models with almost the same scope of supply on the market - in October 2012, however, with price differences of up to 20 €. In this example, the IP camera NC541 / W of the manufacturer Wansview at Amazon for 57 euros was the winner - the technical equivalent, for example, the Foscam FI8908W camera

Commissioning the IP Camera

No matter which camera you choose in this price range, all have in common is that the initial setup according to the will of the manufacturer on Windows is done. A preconfiguration of the camera is necessary, among other things, since this is ex works in its own subnet (192.168.0.X), and the IP address is entered there permanently.

Either you temporarily change the IP address of your computer to use it in this subnet as well, or you can use a Foscam camera tool on Mac OS (www.foscam.de/index.php/foscam-service-and -support / download / viewdownload / 19-software / 15-ip-camera-tool-for-mac), with which you can adjust the IP address of the IP camera. If the camera is unpacked and set up, it basically has the following settings on delivery:

IP address: 192.168.0.178

http: port 80

Username: admin
Password: 123456

For Windows and Mac OS X, use the camera tool to customize the camera's network settings. After the download you start the tool, which then performs a search for the camera in the home network. After a short moment she is already found.

After clicking on the camera found in the home network, a configuration dialog appears in which you can either statically adjust the IP address for your home network or set the check mark in Obtain IP from DHCP server so that the camera automatically sends the dynamic IP address from the camera local DHCP server of the router relates.

Once the IP camera is in the "correct" network, changes will no longer be a problem in the future since the camera has its own administration interface. There, the default password 123456 for the admin user can be changed to a secure password.

In the next step you open the configuration page of the IP camera - simply enter the IP address in the address field of the web browser.

The most important thing is behind you now. The IP camera is now in the same
subnet like the Raspberry Pi running Zoneminder. But a look behind the scenes cannot hurt, maybe there are new opportunities here.

Basically, after signing up, it immediately becomes apparent that the camera offers two different modes depending on the web browser. Mode 1 is for computers with Internet Explorer usage, Mode 2 is for the Firefox, Chrome and Safari competitors. The third option is for mobile devices - in the following, only mode 2 (Firefox, Chrome, Safari) will be used.

First, it checks whether the IP camera is even up to date in terms of firmware and user interface. You can find out in the Maintain tab under Device Status. The language mix is probably due to switching to a different language on the home screen.

In terms of firmware and version of the web interface, it would be nice if you knew if the version used is the current - for lack of a corresponding note in the user interface or in the documents in the box but the Internet must be consulted later.

Now, the first thing to do is to put the camera into operation, however: Basically, in places where an IP camera is to be used, only a suitable RJ45 network socket is available. Thus, the establishment or functioning of the WLAN is the first obligation of a passable wireless LAN IP network camera. Switch to the Network / Wireless Lan area.

Click on the Scan button to check the surrounding area for available WLAN networks. If the suitable wireless network with the matching SSID has been found, mark it and set the corresponding encryption of the WLAN router.

The surprise follows immediately: Here already failed the connection to the wireless router - despite the latest firmware version of the FRITZ! Box router. After several attempts and changes, the cause of this ominous behavior was quickly found: The associated password, ie the key of the WLAN connection, must not contain any special characters in this case.

This is surprising since the use of special characters dramatically increases the security level of such passwords. In this case, however, it means for now: bite into the bullet or waive the wireless feature. If you still have the sour taste in your mouth, the next relevant configuration dialog could cause heartburn in some people already: The adaptation of the dynamic DNS address is anything but user-friendly and confidence-inspiring.

In this dialog, you could enter the dynamic DNS name of the camera if it should be accessible exclusively from the Internet. As a rule, however, this task is already performed by the connected DSL / WLAN router in the home network.

Unclear is the option Do not enable as long as the host name has not been released. Does this mean that errors in DynDNS usage are to be ignored by the camera if the configured DynDNS address is not reachable? In addition, it is unclear when the actual activation of the host name or the release takes place here. Besides, the address 002ndpr.nwsvr.com stands out here. If you search the internet for the domain name nwsvr.com, you'll soon see where this domain hides:

Now everyone should decide for themselves if they want to use this DNS address to control the external access to their IP camera at home.

In this example you should at least remove the entry at Manufacture's Domain and also leave the DynDNS service of the camera switched off first. This is not necessary for zone-minor operation under Raspberry Pi. But in principle, the direct Internet access to the camera for the security-conscious is inadequate: Here, the camera offers no possibilities - neither SSL nor other encryption technologies. So the parsing and reading the data packets including appropriate passwords for the camera access is not a big science, since the unsafe HTTP protocol is used here.

Basically, access to the camera should be controlled via another computer in the home network such as the Raspberry

Pi, or it should be a security solution such as a VPN tunnel o. Ä. "Built around it" to prevent public access to the IP camera.

For operation with zone minors you create a new user in this dialog. In this dialog, it is called raspi and assigned to the user group User. The password used here is raspi123456.

For the Zoneminder project now the essential steps are done - security conscious change nor the default password for the camera admin admin from 123456 to any password. In the next step, add the IP camera to the zone minor configuration and integrate it into the monitor view

Pair IP Camera with Zone Minder

The entry of the IP camera takes place when the zooninder is started via the web front end by clicking on the link Add New Monitor. In this configuration window you first enter a meaningful name for the camera in the General tab under Name. Here the simple term entrance was chosen. For the source type, Remote / Remote is the correct entry, and for Enabled / Enabled, check the box to enable the camera for zone children. In the Source / Source tab, select HTTP for communication from the IP camera to the Raspberry Pi for the transmission protocol.

Here you adapt the host name and, if necessary, the corresponding port for the transmission from the IP camera to the Raspberry Pi.

Depending on the configured port of the IP camera (here: 8088), enter it in Remote Port / Remote Host Port - for the remote host name use the syntax user: password @ <ip-address-of-ip-camera>. If you have created a user (User: raspi, password: raspi123456) to access the IP camera, as in the above example, use the syntax raspi: raspi123456@192.168.123.44 - in this example, 192.168.123.44 is the IP Address of the IP camera in the home network.

With Remote host path / remote path enter /videostream.cgi, for the color depth you use 24-Bit and for the video format first 320 x 240 pixels.

If the devices connected in Zoneminder are configured properly, this is indicated by the color-coded status.

After clicking on the OK button, the IP camera now appears as an additional camera in the zone minor configuration. A moment later, the status of the newly configured camera in the Zoneminder frontend changes to the color of the already confi gurated devices.

Clicking on the montage link in the Zoneminder overview, all camera images of the devices connected to the Raspberry Pi should now appear.

More pixels, more picture quality: In this configuration example, however, we had the condition that the two webcams connected to the Raspberry Pi were configured with a resolution of 320 x 240 pixels - it was only by switching from 640 x 480 pixels to 320 x 240 pixels that the IP could be switched Camera to be co-persuaded to work with the other two local cameras. Obviously, Zoneminder does not support mixed mode of cameras with different image format configuration.

Zone Fine Tuning: More Bandwidth, More Quality

The more cameras are used with the Raspberry Pi and Zoneminder, the more power and bandwidth are needed for smooth playback. Here, the type of use is crucial: Video / image recordings require in this case more I / O resources and less CPU power - a motion detection, however, is comparatively very CPU-heavy and writes less for the SD card.

Using the raspi-config command, you can use the Overclocking command to start the overclocking dialog of the Raspberry Pi. For stability and analysis reasons, you should first start with smaller overclocking steps.

So if you are planning a surveillance system primarily with motion detection (for example, a door viewer), the decent overclocking of the Raspberry Pi brings a perceptible performance kick. Conversely, it pays to buy a larger and faster SD card, if it comes to bumping now and then when saving the files.

Even with longer recordings, it happens that the available space on the Raspberry Pi is not enough. Here you should make sure that the directory / var / cache / zoneminder is sufficiently dimensioned. If you have a NAS server in use on the home network, you can also redirect this zone minor directory (and others) to the network drive via a symbolic link.

Here, the reconfiguration of Zoneminder makes sense to be able to use the storage paths of the home network and the shares available there. Alternatively, you can of course also use remote FTP directories and folders - but these must first be made known on the Raspberry Pi via mount.

Electronic Watchdog On The Raspberry Pi

Whether you operate a locally connected webcam or an IP camera on the Raspberry Pi, both of them can also be configured via Zoneminder as motion detectors and, based on this, they can subsequently do other defined things - for example, notify certain persons or secure the evidence. If Motion Detection is activated in Zoneminder, Zoneminder basically activates the complete camera image.

For example, if you were monitoring your front door, it would also monitor your house ceiling, and depending on the detection sensitivity configured, every fly fall in the image will be reported as a new event - whether or not someone is at the front door. For this reason it makes sense to set a fixed image area for permanently installed cameras for monitoring, not only to avoid false alarms but also to save space for the events.

Basically, every connected camera, which should act as a motion detector, must be reconfigured accordingly. In the Zoneminder main window, select an existing monitor. The following options are available for the function:

Now, if motion detection is switched on by switching to Modect, click on the small, inconspicuous zone link on the right-hand side of the website at the corresponding device. This will take you to the configuration dialog and then define one or more motion detection zones in the image area.

On the right in the image in the Zones column, there is a link behind the number that allows you to specify one or more zones for each device connected and configured with Modect.

Enter a descriptive name for each area that you want to record using motion detection. Here you basically adopt the settings from the following dialog - the configuration Fast, high sensitivity is shot beyond the target for some applications. This even registers the movement of a housefly as a movement - enough reason for you to experiment with the settings.

After aligning the camera, you can simply use the coordinate system of the motion detection grid to specify the corners until exactly the image area to be monitored is selected.

After defining a zone, click the OK button in the configuration window above to return to the initial dialog. If desired, you can configure additional zones for motion detection by clicking on New Zone.

After defining the zone, additional areas to be monitored can be added by clicking the New Zone button.
Less is more: After setting up the zones in the image, the configuration becomes active immediately. Any movement in this area triggers an action and thus costs resources in terms of storage space, CPU and memory load, which are not endlessly available in a Raspberry Pi. For this reason you

should - before you turn up quality and bandwidth here - optimize the settings.

If necessary, consider whether the camera really needs to produce a 24-bit color image or whether a grayscale image is sufficient. In this case, the memory and CPU requirements and thus the transmission bandwidth on the Raspberry Pi would be relieved noticeably. The number of cameras used on the Raspberry Pi also plays a role: More than two devices should not be configured with motion detection activated or even with the recording function in this case.

Better accessible IP cameras over the network are the so-called PTZ cameras, which bring along features such as Pan, Tilt, Zoom (pan, tilt, zoom). Here, the range of services and quality varies depending on the capital employed - but the cheaper price range does not require optical zoom. Whether with or without zoom - with Pan / Tilt support implemented, the Raspberry Pi also lets you use the remote control features of the camera with the Zoneminder installed.

Open the device settings via Zoneminder, there is still no dialog for the control functions of the camera to find.

The remote control functions must first be activated explicitly with the zone-minor options in the system register with a check mark in OPT_CONTROL. After the zoneminder restart via service zoneminder restart, Zoneminder is available for the PTZ function.
After ticking, Zoneminder points out that changes will only become active after the restart.

Zoneminder already includes a small set of preconfigured controllable PTZ cameras in the basic installation, each of which can be found as a Perl module in the directory / usr / share / perl5 / ZoneMinder / Control /. If necessary, a suitable control module is included for your camera - to find out, the Zoneminder Wiki (www.zoneminder.com/wiki/) is a good place to start.

Conclusion

Thank you for making it through to the end of *Raspberry Pi 4: Project Ideas Book*, let's hope it was informative and able to provide you with all of the tools you need to achieve your goals whatever they may be.

One of the central goals of the creation of Raspberry Pi was the educational end - to provide children with an early interest in computing and programming. Hence the Raspbian base installation includes Scratch and Python, two interesting ways to enhance programming language learning.

Raspberry Pi is not just about the operating system, so the app store - the Pi Store - was recently launched.

One of Pi Store's goals is to motivate young people to create programs and monetize them, as not all downloadable resources are free.

Among the dozens of resources available is the free office application suite, the CodeBlocks programming IDE, and Open Arena, a game based on the Quake III game engine.

What Is It Possible To Do With A Raspberry Pi?

Although initially developed for educational purposes, innovative and interesting projects have been emerging over the last few months, using this micro-computer as a starting point:

- Arcade game machine

- Musical instrument
- Computer cluster
- SmartTV
- Home automation
- Media Center

We hope this book gave you a better insight into Raspberry Pi and how you can have fun with this amazing program.

Finally, if you found this book useful in any way, a review on Amazon is always appreciated!

Description

In recent years, two platforms have gained immense popularity in the electronics world. Thanks to Raspberry Pi, everyone can start creating interesting electronic projects! This book will introduce everyone to this extremely popular single-board computer.

What Is Raspberry Pi?

Raspberry Pi is the most popular mini credit card size computer in the world! Thanks to the relatively low price and huge possibilities, it quickly gained millions of fans. On a small board, we can find among others 4-core processor, RAM, USB, Internet, and HDMI connections. The latest version (used in the course) is also equipped with a WiFi and Bluetooth module.

In addition, the board has universal GPIO terminals to which various electronic components can be connected (eg diodes, buttons, sensors). The producer has also prepared a connector through which a camera can be connected to the popular Raspberry Pi.

Raspberry Pi is a small computer with outputs that allows easy connection of electronic components, eg temperature sensor.

Who Is The Raspberry Pi Book For?

The book has been prepared for everyone. No knowledge of Raspberry Pi, programming, or Linux systems is required. Knowledge of basic electronics concepts is welcome, but not a prerequisite!

Rasberry Pi has numerous applications! To take advantage of the possibilities that a Raspberry offers us, you need to take the first step and learn the basics of working with this computer. This book begins with Raspberry Pi's complete fundamentals: from system installation (in many ways), through necessary configurations and expert use of Linux, to universal GPIO ports.

So order your copy and start learning today!!!

Made in the USA
Columbia, SC
18 February 2021